CHRISTIAN THEOLOGY

THE BASICS

Christian Theology: The Basics is a concise introduction to the nature, questions and central concerns of theology – the study of God within the Christian tradition. Providing a broad overview of the story that Christianity tells us about our human situation before God, this book will also seek to provide encouragement and a solid foundation for the reader's further explorations within the subject. With debates surrounding the relation between faith and reason in theology, the book opens with a consideration of the basis of theology and goes on to explore key topics including:

- The identity of Jesus and debates in Christology
- The role of the Bible in shaping theological inquiry
- The centrality of the Trinity for all forms of Christian thinking
- The promise of salvation and how it is achieved.

With suggestions for further reading at the end of each chapter, along with a glossary, *Christian Theology: The Basics* is the ideal starting point for those new to the study of theology.

Murray Rae is Professor of Theology at the University of Otago, New Zealand.

The Basics

ACTING
BELLA MERLIN

AMERICAN PHILOSOPHY
NANCY STANLICK

ANCIENT NEAR EAST
DANIEL C. SNELL

ANTHROPOLOGY
PETER METCALF

ARCHAEOLOGY (SECOND EDITION)
CLIVE GAMBLE

ART HISTORY
GRANT POOKE AND
DIANA NEWALL

ARTIFICIAL INTELLIGENCE
KEVIN WARWICK

THE BIBLE
JOHN BARTON

BIOETHICS
ALASTAIR V. CAMPBELL

BUDDHISM
CATHY CANTWELL

THE CITY
KEVIN ARCHER

CONTEMPORARY LITERATURE
SUMAN GUPTA

CRIMINAL LAW
JONATHAN HERRING

CRIMINOLOGY (SECOND EDITION)
SANDRA WALKLATE

DANCE STUDIES
JO BUTTERWORTH

EASTERN PHILOSOPHY
VICTORIA S. HARRISON

ECONOMICS (THIRD EDITION)
TONY CLEAVER

EDUCATION
KAY WOOD

ENERGY
MICHAEL SCHOBERT

EUROPEAN UNION (SECOND EDITION)
ALEX WARLEIGH-LACK

EVOLUTION
SHERRIE LYONS

FILM STUDIES (SECOND EDITION)
AMY VILLAREJO

FINANCE (SECOND EDITION)
ERIK BANKS

FREE WILL
MEGHAN GRIFFITH

GENDER
HILARY LIPS

GLOBAL MIGRATION
BERNADETTE HANLON
AND THOMAS VICINIO

HUMAN GENETICS
RICKI LEWIS

HUMAN GEOGRAPHY
ANDREW JONES

INTERNATIONAL RELATIONS
PETER SUTCH AND JUANITA ELIAS

ISLAM (SECOND EDITION)
COLIN TURNER

JOURNALISM STUDIES
MARTIN CONBOY

JUDAISM
JACOB NEUSNER

LANGUAGE (SECOND EDITION)
R. L. TRASK

LAW
GARY SLAPPER AND DAVID KELLY

LITERARY THEORY (THIRD EDITION)
HANS BERTENS

LOGIC
JC BEALL

MANAGEMENT
MORGEN WITZEL

MARKETING (SECOND EDITION)
KARL MOORE AND NIKETH PAREEK

MEDIA STUDIES
JULIAN MCDOUGALL

METAPHYSICS
MICHAEL REA

THE OLYMPICS
ANDY MIAH AND BEATRIZ GARCIA

PHILOSOPHY (FIFTH EDITION)
NIGEL WARBURTON

PHYSICAL GEOGRAPHY
JOSEPH HOLDEN

POETRY (SECOND EDITION)
JEFFREY WAINWRIGHT

POLITICS (FIFTH EDITION)
STEPHEN TANSEY AND NIGEL JACKSON

PUBLIC RELATIONS
RON SMITH

THE QUR'AN
MASSIMO CAMPANINI

RACE AND ETHNICITY
PETER KIVISTO AND PAUL R. CROLL

RELIGION (SECOND EDITION)
MALORY NYE

RELIGION AND SCIENCE
PHILIP CLAYTON

RESEARCH METHODS
NICHOLAS WALLIMAN

ROMAN CATHOLICISM
MICHAEL WALSH

SEMIOTICS (SECOND EDITION)
DANIEL CHANDLER

SHAKESPEARE (THIRD EDITION)
SEAN MCEVOY

SOCIAL WORK
MARK DOEL

SOCIOLOGY
KEN PLUMMER

SPECIAL EDUCATIONAL NEEDS
JANICE WEARMOUTH

SUBCULTURES
ROSS HAENFLER

SUSTAINABILITY
PETER JACQUES

TELEVISION STUDIES
TOBY MILLER

TERRORISM
JAMES LUTZ AND BRENDA LUTZ

THEATRE STUDIES (SECOND EDITION)
ROBERT LEACH

WOMEN'S STUDIES
BONNIE SMITH

WORLD HISTORY
PETER N. STEARNS

CHRISTIAN THEOLOGY

THE BASICS

Murray Rae

Routledge
Taylor & Francis Group

LONDON AND NEW YORK

First published 2015
by Routledge
2 Park Square, Milton Park, Abingdon, Oxon OX14 4RN

and by Routledge
711 Third Avenue, New York, NY 10017

Routledge is an imprint of the Taylor & Francis Group, an informa business

British Library Cataloguing in Publication Data
A catalogue record for this book is available from the British Library

Library of Congress Cataloging in Publication Data
Rae, Murray.
Christian theology : the basics / Murray Rae. -- 1 [edition].
pages cm. -- (The basics)
Includes bibliographical references and index.
1. Theology, Doctrinal--Popular works. 2. Theology. I. Title.
BT77.R25 2015
230--dc23
2014037953

ISBN: 978-0-415-81495-9 (hbk)
ISBN: 978-0-415-81494-2 (pbk)
ISBN: 978-1-315-73026-4 (ebk)

Typeset in Bembo
by Taylor & Francis Books

CONTENTS

Preface   viii

1 Speaking of God   1
2 Creation and Covenant   23
3 Jesus and the Spirit   43
4 The Triune God   70
5 Salvation   89
6 Christian Hope   113
7 A New Community   138

   Glossary   160
   Bibliography   170
   Index   175

PREFACE

The subject matter of Christian theology is the God who meets us in Jesus of Nazareth. That God is the same God who created all things, who called and formed Israel to be the bearer of his promise that all the families of the earth should be blessed, and who brings that promise to fulfilment through Jesus Christ and through the Spirit. Christian theology goes about its work in light of this reality and in attentiveness to it. It deals, therefore, with something that is given. It deals with God's gift of himself as creator, redeemer and sustainer of all that is.

This account of what Christian theology is arises from a long history, beginning with Israel and continuing through the life of the Christian church. In order to understand the content of Christian theology, it is necessary to develop some familiarity with that history, particularly as it is told in the Bible. The Bible is a collection of many different kinds of literature, including historical narrative, but including as well prayers, laments, parables, laws, theological reflections and so on. It is a literature, so Christians believe, that was called forth by God, that bears witness to God's gift of himself, and that becomes, again and again, an instrument through which God makes himself known. It is for this reason that the Bible is the primary source and authority for the work of Christian theology. The Bible is also, therefore, the primary source and authority for this book. As you read the chapters that follow, it will be helpful to have the Bible at hand. It would be helpful too, if you have not done so already, to familiarise yourself with some of the Bible's content. Begin by reading one of the gospels, Matthew, Mark, Luke or John, and, from the Old Testament, the books of Genesis and Exodus, which give a good orientation to the central elements of Israel's story.

Alongside the frequent reference to biblical texts, this book will also introduce beginners in the field of Christian theology to some of the terminology that theology commonly uses. Wherever possible, the meanings of theological terms are explained within the text, but readers are also referred to a glossary of terms, movements and events that can be found on pp. 160–169.

There are various ways in which the content of Christian theology could be presented in a book such as this. I have chosen to organise the chapters around major themes of Christian theology, beginning with Revelation and proceeding then to discuss God's work in Creation and Covenant, Jesus and the Spirit, the Trinity, Salvation, Christian Hope and then, finally, the church. Although the Spirit appears in the title of chapter three, discussion of the Spirit is in fact woven through the whole book and rises to prominence in several chapters. Likewise, there is no chapter dedicated explicitly to humanity, but, again, this theme appears in all chapters, while receiving particular attention in chapter two.

While the organisation and content of a book such as this reflects the theological convictions of the author, it also reflects the author's particular cultural and ecclesial context. Those with a trained eye will recognise in the content of this book that I belong to the Reformed theological tradition as it has developed in a Western cultural context. That shapes every sentence that is found in this book, but I have tried wherever possible to draw upon wider traditions, and to point readers in the direction of further reading that should be done in order to appreciate the rich diversity and breadth of Christian theology. I hope, however, to have introduced readers to the central content of Christian theology, and to have done so in a way that will encourage further exploration.

There are many people whose own theological work and Christian faith have enriched and encouraged my own – far too many to mention here. I am especially grateful, however, to Lucy

Peppiatt, Principal of Westminster Theological Centre in the UK, who read early chapters of this work and provided helpful and encouraging feedback. I am grateful too for the assistance given by Iram Satti at Taylor & Francis in bringing this book to production.

SPEAKING OF GOD

The task of theology is to speak of God. That is what the word 'theology' means. Combining the two Greek terms *Theos* (God) and *logos* (word), theology is simply speech about God. But how is the theologian to go about this task? On what basis is it possible for human beings to say anything at all about the subject matter of theology? That is a matter of debate among theologians, but the approach taken in this book is that theology is possible only on the basis that God has spoken to humankind. God has given himself to be known, through the history of Israel, and supremely in the person of Jesus Christ. Put another way, theologians take their clues about what may be said about God from what God has revealed of himself.

There was a time, so the story goes, when a man named Abram heard a voice from the Lord saying, 'Go from your country and your kindred and your father's house to the land that I will show you. I will make of you a great nation, and I will bless you, and make your name great, so that you will be a blessing. I will bless those who bless you, and the one who curses you, I will curse, and in you all the families of the earth will be blessed' (Genesis 12:1–3). Thus begins a story Israel tells of its dealings with God. It is a story told by prophets and kings, shepherd boys and maidservants. It winds its way through a long history of struggle and calamity, triumph and defeat, despair and promise, until at last it comes to the man Jesus, of whom it is said, God has spoken to us now by a Son (Hebrews 1:2).

Christian theology is the thinking and speaking done in the light of this story, most especially by those who participate in it. Although the term 'theology' as used in this book will refer particularly to Christian theology, it will become clear that Christian theology has its roots in and remains deeply entwined with and dependent upon Israel's theology. Jesus was an Israelite. He was born of David's line. The God who speaks through him, as the letter to the Hebrews puts it, is the God of Abraham and Isaac, Rebecca and Naomi, Moses and Jeremiah and Ruth. To say this is to make a far-reaching theological claim not only about the nature and being of God, but also about the way theology must proceed. The God of Christian faith reveals himself to a particular people and through a particular history. We are not dealing in theology with abstract concepts, with a philosophical system, or with a spirituality developed from within the self. We are dealing with a God who involves himself in history as its Creator, Redeemer and Sustainer. Theology is a matter of attentiveness to what this God does. It involves attentiveness to what theologians call the divine economy.

> The 'divine economy' is a term used to describe all that God does in relation to the world. This activity of God is distinguished from the internal relations of Father, Son and Spirit.

THEOLOGY AS WITNESS

Christian theology thus begins with the recognition that God acts, that God reveals himself, that God has spoken through the prophets and, in these last days, through a Son. The letter to the Hebrews goes on to say that this Son is the reflection of God's glory and the exact imprint of God's very being, and that he sustains all things by his powerful word (Hebrews 1:3). We will return to these claims in chapter three when we speak in more detail about the person of Christ, but for now, it is important simply to note the form that Christian theological claims take. They are, first of all, a witness to what God has done. We see this in the testimony offered by the author of the letter to the Hebrews: 'in these last days God has spoken through a Son'.

Drawing upon the biblical witness, the creeds of the church testify that 'Jesus Christ, [God's] only Son, our Lord, was conceived by the Holy Spirit, born of the virgin Mary, suffered under Pontius Pilate, was crucified, died and was buried ... ' and so on. These claims offer further description of what God has done. As with all historical testimony, however, these claims, along with many others in the Bible, are infused with interpretative judgements. They attempt to explain not only what has happened, but also what these things mean. So, for example, Jesus, the Son of Mary and of Joseph, is confessed to be the Christ, the long-awaited Messiah who fulfils the promises once delivered to Israel and inaugurates the coming kingdom of God. His crucifixion and his resurrection from the dead are said to be for the forgiveness of sins. We see here, added to the witness, a confession about what these events of history mean and to what end they are directed. Theological speech, Christianly understood, ought always to have this character of witness and of confession.

> The church has occasionally formulated short statements of Christian faith that are known as 'creeds', from the Latin word *credo*, 'I believe'. The most important of these are the Apostles' Creed, probably written during the second century AD, and the fourth-century Nicene Creed.

Several implications follow from this claim. Because theological speech has the character of witness, it always points beyond itself to a reality that it cannot replace. Theological speech points in the direction of the divine reality. Just as the angels, the bearers of good news, said to the women on Easter morning, 'come and see the place where Jesus lay' (Matthew 28:6), theological speech invites its hearers to 'come and see' for themselves where God is at work in the world. Theological speech cannot stand in for the reality itself. It can only gesture towards the reality of God's self-disclosure which, in the end, must be allowed to speak for itself.

THEOLOGICAL LANGUAGE

A second implication is that there is always a provisionality and an inadequacy about theological speech. Our language certainly cannot exhaust or encapsulate the reality of God. God may reveal himself through the language of Christian witness, but he is not tethered by it. Some readers will have detected already the inadequacy of theological speech. I have been using a personal, masculine pronoun to refer to God. This practice is appropriate insofar as it indicates that God is personal, but wholly inappropriate in its suggestion that God is male. Unfortunately, the English language does not have any personal pronouns available that are not gendered. We could use 'it', but that would render God an object at our disposal rather than the personal God who encounters us as subjects. I have chosen to persist, therefore, with inadequate male pronouns in order to bear witness to the *personal* character of God. My choice of male rather than female personal pronouns is shaped also by convention. Some, understandably, find that jarring; I acknowledge the difficulty that it causes but, in my judgement, the abandonment of personal pronouns gives away too much, while the adoption of female pronouns reads more gender, not less, into the being of God. Others in the tradition of Christian theology make a different judgement and adopt different practices. The debate highlights the inadequacy of our language about God.

Despite this inadequacy, however, the language of theological witness has succeeded again and again in engendering and nurturing faith. To what might this success be attributed? We have first to consider what faith is. Faith is a form of life lived in response to God's action. We will be more specific in subsequent chapters about what God's action consists in and about the form of life it calls for. For the moment, though, let us note that faith is a response to divine initiative. It is consequent upon God's action. Insofar, then, that theological speech has succeeded again and again in engendering and nurturing faith, it must be seen as participating somehow in this divine initiative. Theological speech, we might say, is called forth and enlivened by God. This is said especially of the theological witness of Scripture. The theological claim made here is that Scripture is inspired. This does not mean that Scripture is not a human witness. We know much about the circumstances of its production and transmission, and we can see the ways it has been shaped by human interests and by human understanding, but people of faith testify that through the words of Scripture they are encountered by God; they hear the voice of God, and they are drawn to share in Scripture's account of how and where God is at work in the world.

To inspire means to give breath, to enliven. The same root of this word in Hebrew (*ruach*), in Greek (*pneuma*) and in English is also used of the Spirit. According to biblical understanding, therefore, the words of Scripture are given life by the Spirit. Through the Spirit, God calls forth the witness of Scripture, makes eloquent the stumbling testimony of human authors and, through their testimony, gives himself to be known. It is for this reason that Scripture is regarded as the primary source of Christian theology. There are other sources too – experience, reason and the tradition of the church are those usually acknowledged – but in the approach to Christian theology taken in this book, these have a relative authority. They are subordinate to the authority of Scripture. We will shortly consider some other approaches that accord primary authority to reason, to the church and its tradition, or to experience. But first, let us consider the authority of Scripture.

THE WITNESS OF SCRIPTURE

The great Protestant Reformer John Calvin (1509–64) claimed that 'no one can get even the slightest taste of right and sound doctrine unless he be a pupil of Scripture' (Calvin, *Institutes of the Christian Religion*, Book I, ch. VI.2). This is a conviction championed especially by the Protestant Reformers, but all branches of the Christian church recognise that theology is both enabled by and, in a certain, positive sense, constrained by Scripture. Theology is *enabled* by Scripture because it is in Scripture that the story is told of God's engagement with the world, culminating in the life, death and resurrection of Jesus Christ. Christian theology, as has been suggested above, is the thinking done in light of that story. Theology is *constrained* by Scripture in the sense that the story Scripture tells provides the essential content of Christian theology. This constraint means that Christian theologians are not free, as theologians, to tell some other story that is incompatible with the story Scripture tells, but it also means that Christian theology has a definite and positive content and that theologians are not left to their own devices when they attempt to speak of God.

The 'story' Scripture tells is not a singular historical account of God's engagement with the world. The various writings that are gathered together in Scripture include historical narratives, but also laws, prayers, songs, poetry, parables, proverbs and so on. Alongside and woven into the narratives about what God has said and done, we find the responses of God's people in prayer and praise, in theological interpretation of what it all means, and in ethical reflection about what form of life is called forth and enabled by God's action. The biblical authors were themselves theologians, observing, responding to and trying to make sense of what God is doing in the world. It is important to note that the biblical writers are not all of one mind. They share a commitment, it appears, to speak of God and God's purposes as they have been revealed through Israel, but they do not always agree on what God requires of them. Was it necessary, for example, for Israel to maintain racial purity in order to fulfill God's calling upon them to be his people? Ezra and Nehemiah thought it was and so advised against intermarriage with other races, but the author of Ruth clearly had another view and so tells the story of how King David, Israel's greatest king, was the great-grandson of Ruth, a Moabite woman who had married the Israelite Boaz. Or again, at various stages of the biblical story there is a difference of opinion about whether a temple is needed in order to worship and honour God. David proposed that a temple should be built but was advised against it (2 Samuel 7:1–7). Later in the story, Solomon receives God's blessing for his plans to build a temple. Later still, after the temple is destroyed and Israel finds itself in exile, the question is raised whether Israel can worship God in a foreign land, without the possibility of fulfilling the annual cycle of festivals and sacrifices in the temple. Jesus, who at several points in his life appears to honour the temple (e.g. Luke 2:41–49; John 2:13–17), then seems to be indifferent to its possible destruction (John 2:18–22). The need for a temple and its role within Israel's relationship with God is a matter of ongoing debate and disagreement that extends into the New Testament.

Given the rich diversity of the biblical witness, the multiple genres employed by its authors and the searching theological enquiries that reveal contrasting points of view, the authority of Scripture must be carefully conceived. Its authority is not honoured by extracting 'proof-texts' to support a particular theological position.

The authority of Scripture rests, rather, in the use God makes of it to communicate with his people. Reading Scripture is a discipline requiring discernment, faithfulness, wisdom, obedience. It is the discipline through which the people of God learn to be attentive to God's voice. They are schooled in this discipline by the Lord himself, as is apparent especially in the conversation Jesus has with his disciples on the road to Emmaus following his resurrection (see Luke 24:27). Jesus' interpretation of the Scriptures in this incident reveals an important principle for all Christian reading of Scripture. It is to be read under the guidance of God and in attentiveness to his voice. For this reason, reading Scripture as a source for theology, as a source, that is, for Christian reflection upon who God is and what God does, ought to take place in the context of prayer.

An ancient saying of the church, possibly originating with Prosper of Aquitaine, a Christian writer of the early fifth century, reads *lex orandi, lex credendi*. The Latin phrase, translated 'the law of praying is the law of believing', suggests that understanding or belief comes through prayer. As it is with theology in general, so also with the reading of Scripture: understanding depends upon God's help. That help is sought through prayer. It is also sought through participation in the community that gathers around Scripture to partake in fellowship with the one whom Scripture calls Lord and to attend to his Word. The reading of Scripture for theological understanding is ultimately a task of the community of faith, of that community that knows itself to be addressed and equipped and commissioned by God for the tasks of worship, of witness and of faithful service. That community is called the church. It is possible to read the texts gathered together in the Bible apart from the community of faith and to treat the Bible as something other than a mode of God's communication with his people. But in this case the reader is no longer engaged in the task of Christian theology. The authority of Scripture for theology rests in the fact that God in person speaks through it. The theologian's task, accordingly, is to be attentive to the *viva vox Dei*, the living voice of God.

TRADITION

The theologian does not work alone in giving attention to the voice of God. There is a community, extended across time and space, that is devoted to the same task. This community, as we have just observed, is the church. Under the headship of Christ and the guidance of the Spirit, this community has learned things about the nature and purpose of God that have an enduring value. The theologian does well, therefore, to attend not only to Scripture but also to the insight given to the church down through the ages and across the vast expanse of the church's present life. A recent example is the contribution made to theology by Christians within the Pentecostal and Charismatic movements who have drawn attention to features of the biblical witness, particularly concerning the role of the Holy Spirit, that other branches of the church have tended to overlook. In the late twentieth and early twenty-first centuries there has been a major shift in the location of the Christian population away from the West and towards Africa, Asia and Latin America. As the gospel is increasingly taken up and refracted through the lenses of non-Western cultures, new insights emerge into the content of Scripture. The work of theologians, and indeed of the whole church, is enriched by this expansion of insight into the biblical text.

> The Protestant Reformation began in 1517 with a dispute about key elements of Christian teaching. The theological dispute eventually led to many Christians in Western Europe leaving the Roman Catholic Church and establishing new churches that were no longer tied to Rome.

Alongside the enrichment and insight provided through attentiveness to the wide diversity of perspectives found in the Christian church, theology is guided and enriched through attention to the long history of Christian reflection upon the biblical witness. The accumulated findings of this history of theological reflection as affirmed and taught by the church are together called the 'tradition'. This tradition is regarded as a secondary source of authority for theological enquiry. Precisely how much authority should be accorded to tradition is, however, a matter of disagreement between various branches of the Christian church. The Roman Catholic Church places a high value on the authority of tradition and the teaching of the church and ranks the church's interpretation of Scripture as equivalent in authority to

Scripture itself. Protestant churches, on the other hand, regard the authority of tradition as subordinate to that of Scripture. Martin Luther (1483–1546), for instance, who was the prime instigator of the Protestant Reformation, argued that he would stand by his understanding of justification even though it differed from the account given by the church and that he would renounce it only if it could be shown to be in conflict with Scripture. At the Council of Trent that met from 1545–63 in response to Luther and to the Protestant Reformation more broadly, the Roman Catholic Church offered the following statement of its position:

> Following, then, the examples of the orthodox Fathers, [the holy, ecumenical and general Council of Trent] receives and venerates with a feeling of piety and reverence all the books both of the Old and New Testaments, since one God is the author of both; also the traditions, whether they relate to faith or to morals, as having been dictated either orally by Christ or by the Holy Ghost, and preserved in the Catholic Church in unbroken succession.
>
> (*Documents of the Council of Trent*, Session IV)

Meeting in the 1960s, the Second Vatican Council of the Roman Catholic Church reiterated this view:

> ... both sacred tradition and sacred Scripture are to be accepted and venerated with the same sense of devotion and reverence. Sacred tradition and sacred Scripture form one sacred deposit of the word of God, which is committed to the Church ... It is clear, therefore, that sacred tradition, sacred Scripture and the teaching authority of the Church, in accord with God's most wise design, are so linked and joined together that one cannot stand without the others, and that all together and each in its own way under the action of the one Holy Spirit contribute effectively to the salvation of souls.
>
> ('Dogmatic Constitution on Divine Revelation' (*Dei Verbum*),
> *Documents of Vatican II*, par. 9, 10, 21)

Appeals to tradition began to appear very early in Christian history. The apostle Paul makes such an appeal when he writes to the church in Corinth, saying, 'For I received from the Lord, what I also handed on to you ... ' The word 'tradition' comes from the Latin *traditio*, meaning to hand over. So Paul is here handing over or passing on a teaching that he has received. Within the early church, similarly, there emerged a body of teaching passed on both orally and in writing that was said to have been received from the apostles. So, for example, the second-century theologian Irenaeus (*c*.130– *c*.202) writes, 'The Church, though dispersed through the whole world, even to the ends of the earth, has received from the apostles and their disciples this faith … ' (Irenaeus, *Against Heresies*, Book I, ch. 10). Irenaeus then proceeds to offer a summative description of what the church believes, often called the 'rule of faith', before adding that no one who is a ruler in the churches will teach doctrines different from these. The 'rule of faith' does not refer to a single authorised statement of belief, such as the Nicene or Apostles' Creed, but rather to the central tenets of orthodox Christian belief. The 'rule of faith', developed through tradition, maps out the conceptual territory within which Christian theology goes about its work.

As the body of Christian reflection on Scripture accumulated, appeals to tradition became common in theological argument. The Council of Chalcedon in 451, for example, began its famous affirmation of the two natures of Christ with the words 'Therefore, following the holy fathers, we all with one voice confess our Lord Jesus Christ to be one and the same Son, perfect in divinity and humanity, truly God and truly human … ' The claim to be 'following the holy fathers' added considerable weight, so the Council assumed, to its own theological formulations. It remains important in the Eastern Orthodox tradition in particular that the church's theology should conform to that developed 'by the holy fathers' in the period extending roughly from the New Testament to the Council of Chalcedon in 451.

During the course of its life the church has sometimes called Councils to resolve theological disputes and to discuss other matters concerning the life of the church. From the fourth to the ninth century there were seven such Councils. Because they are widely, though not universally, regarded as authoritative for the church worldwide, these seven are known as ecumenical Councils. The Council of Chalcedon that met in 451 is one of these.

Appeals to the tradition or to the teaching of the church served well in theological disputation throughout the Middle Ages, but at the time of the Protestant Reformation, the Reformers found themselves taking issue with some aspects of the received teaching of the church. Within Protestant theology, accordingly, Scripture was elevated above tradition and, as interpreted to us by the Holy Spirit, was confessed to be the 'supreme authority' for all matters of faith and life. John Calvin thus writes: 'Let this be a firm principle: No other word is to be held as the Word of God, and given place as such in the church, than what is contained first in the Law and the Prophets, then in the writings of the apostles; and the only authorised way of teaching in the church is by the prescription and standard of his Word' (Calvin, *Institutes of the Christian Religion*, Book IV, ch. VIII.8).

Calvin has no wish to reject the authority of tradition. He explains elsewhere that 'we willingly embrace and reverence as holy the early Councils, such as those of Nicaea, Constantinople, Ephesus 1, Chalcedon, and the like … ' (Calvin, *Institutes*, Book IV, ch. VIII.8), but he insists that the deliberations of all Councils, along with all church pronouncements, must be 'examined by the standard of Scripture' (Calvin, *Institutes*, Book IV, ch. VIII.8). The authority of church and tradition is a subordinate authority that is always open to challenge. The Thirty-Nine Articles confirmed by the Anglican Church in 1563 offer a similar view, stating, 'Wherefore things ordained by [General Councils] as necessary to salvation have neither strength not authority, unless it may be declared that they be taken out of Holy Scripture' (Article XXI, taken from *The Book of Common Prayer*).

An Eastern Orthodox Council meeting in Jerusalem in 1672 responded to the Reformation disputes over the authority of tradition with a position closely aligned to the Roman Catholic view. That Council stated that 'the witness of the Catholic Church is, we believe, not of inferior authority to that of the Divine Scriptures'. The term 'Catholic' in this context means the universal church, rather than the Roman Catholic Church. The basis for this confidence, according to the Council, is that the Holy Spirit is the author of both the Scriptures and the church. It is 'quite the same' therefore 'to be taught by the Scriptures and by the Catholic Church' ('Confession of Dositheus, Or, The Acts of the Synod of Jerusalem, 1692', Decree II).

While most branches of the Christian church uphold a view of the authority of tradition somewhere within the range outlined above, there have been some rare cases of theologians who have denied any authority to tradition or to the teaching of the church. Some of the so-called radical Reformers, like the Anabaptist Balthasar Hubmaier (c.1480–1528), appeared to draw close to such a view in their polemic against the church of Rome. A more extreme view still is expressed by Alexander Campbell (1788–1866), a minister of the Restoration Movement in the United States, who said,

> I have endeavored to read the Scriptures as though no one had read them before me, and I am as much on my guard against reading them today, through the medium of my own views yesterday, or a week ago, as I am against being influenced by any foreign name, authority, or system whatever.
> (Alexander Campbell, 'Reply [to Robert Baylor Semple]', in *Christian Baptist* 3 (April 3, 1826), p. 229)

Most theologians recognise, however, that there is much to be learned from those who have preceded them in seeking to be attentive to the Word of God in Scripture. The principal point of disagreement concerns the degree of authority that should be accorded to that tradition. Does tradition have an authority equal to Scripture or subordinate to it? On that question the Protestant churches have tended to diverge from the Roman Catholic and the Orthodox, but whatever degree of authority is accorded to tradition, an account must be given of how that authority is established. The most common view is that the authority of tradition is based on apostolic succession. For the Roman Catholic and the Orthodox, apostolic succession refers primarily to an unbroken line of episcopal ordination through the laying-on of hands. Authority is passed on through the succession of bishops who preserve in the church a body of unwritten teaching of the apostles that complements the scriptural witness. The Orthodox churches emphasise as well the role of the liturgy in preserving this tradition. Protestants, on the other hand, are more inclined to attribute the authority of tradition to the providential work of the Spirit in preserving the gospel through the teaching of the church. The test of the church's teaching, however, is always its conformity to Scripture. It can claim no authority independent of the written Word.

REASON

The prerogative claimed by the Protestant Reformers to challenge tradition in the light of Scripture helped sow the seeds of a similarly momentous shift in the contours of Western culture. This cultural shift is known as the Enlightenment. Prompted in part by the Copernican revolution, in which traditional views of the structure of the universe were overturned, the Enlightenment set about divesting itself of any reliance upon tradition. The traditional view had been that Earth was the centre of the solar system and the sun and all the planets revolved around it. That is what appears to happen as we see the sun rise in the east, move across the sky and set in the west, but the investigations of scientists like Copernicus and Galileo demonstrated that this traditional, common-sense view was wrong. Tradition had been shown to be untrustworthy, at least in this matter, and so the authority of tradition more generally was thrown into doubt. People increasingly adopted the view that the only way to be sure of our claims about the world was to subject them to the scrutiny of scientific reason. From this flowed the view that our investigation of reality should be detached and objective and should not rely on any supposed wisdom received from traditional authorities like the Bible or the church. The French mathematician René Descartes (1596–1650), who was one of the key thinkers of the Enlightenment, set himself the task of finding a sure basis for all human truth claims and determined to begin by wiping the slate clean, by abandoning all the beliefs he had previously held, and by accepting as true only that which his reason could confirm beyond any shadow of a doubt. Descartes himself remained a Christian and thought that reason could prove the existence of God, but some who followed him became convinced that belief in God was defeated by rational thought. Whatever conclusion one drew on this matter, the Enlightenment had set human reason firmly in a position of authority superior to that of the church and of Scripture. As epitomised in the title of Immanuel Kant's work *Religion Within the Limits of Reason Alone,* published in German in 1793, theology, it was supposed, was obliged to serve a new master.

Despite numerous fateful consequences of this elevation of human reason, not least the considerable impetus given to individualistic conceptions of our humanity, it was not an entirely new idea that human reason should be regarded as authoritative for theology. Very early in the history of the church, there were theologians who contended that the Christian gospel ought to be proclaimed in ways that were intelligible to rational thought. The so-called Apologists of the second century, including theologians like Aristides, Justin Martyr and Theophilus of Antioch, set out to offer a rational defence of Christian faith in the face of philosophical objections. While they certainly appealed to Scripture, they also appealed to reason in defence of their theological convictions. Clement of Alexandria (*c*.150–*c*.215) is another theologian of the late second century who had a high regard for Greek philosophy and its tradition of rational thought. He drew upon the Platonic and Stoic traditions in order to clarify and explain aspects of Christian faith and described philosophy as 'the handmaid of theology'. 'Philosophy', says Clement, 'was a preparation, paving the way for him who is perfected in Christ' (Clement of Alexandria, *The Stromata*, 1.5).

Others, however, were much less sure that reason could be pressed so easily into the service of faith. Clement's contemporary, Tertullian (160–220), a North African lawyer turned theologian, rebuked the effort to reconcile Greek philosophy with Christian faith by scornfully enquiring, 'What indeed has Athens to do with Jerusalem? What concord is there between the Academy and the Church?' Tertullian continues, 'We want no curious disputation after possessing Christ Jesus, no inquisition after enjoying the gospel! With our faith, we desire no further belief' (Tertullian, *On Prescription Against Heretics*, vii). In support of his disdain for philosophy, Tertullian cites the apostle Paul, who writes in the letter to the Colossians, 'See to it that no one takes you captive through philosophy and empty deceit, according to human tradition … ' (Colossians 2:8), and in 1 Corinthians: 'For the wisdom of this world is foolishness with God' (1 Corinthians 3:19). To be sure, Tertullian's tirade is directed against pagan philosophy rather than against reason in general, but the errors of philosophy indicate, in Tertullian's view, the unreliability of reason as a source of truth. It is important to note that Tertullian himself was a fine exponent of reasoned argument. He does not oppose the use of reason as a tool, but it has no authority when left to its own devices; it must be tutored by revelation, or by the teaching of the apostles. Tertullian's preference for the teaching of the apostles over philosophical reasoning safeguards an important characteristic of Christian faith, namely that it is available to all and is not restricted to the cultured or to the highly educated. It is not made accessible through some sophisticated intellectual argument which, in Tertullian's view, is more likely to mislead than inform.

Tertullian's suspicion of reason notwithstanding, the theological tradition as it developed through the course of the Middle Ages generally adopted a more conciliatory view of the relation between reason and faith. Thomas Aquinas (1225–74), the most influential theologian of the late medieval era, regarded reason as a competent source of understanding that could yield a knowledge of truth that was compatible with revelation and indeed supported it. Nevertheless, there are some truths of theology, Aquinas suggests, that lie beyond reason's grasp and for which we must rely on faith. Faith is therefore described as being 'above reason'; it is a superior authority and gives access to things that 'surpass all understanding' (Aquinas, *Summa Contra Gentiles*, Book 1, ch. V). Aquinas also sets forth the interesting argument that while a good deal of theological truth is in principle accessible to reason, not all people are capable of the strenuous effort required to attain the truth through reason. Some do not have the intellectual capacity, some are too busy with other concerns, and some are simply too lazy. For this reason, God, who desires that 'all should share in the knowledge of God easily, and without doubt or error', offers understanding to all through faith (Aquinas, *Summa Contra Gentiles*, Book 1, ch. IV). Aquinas thus echoes Clement's positive appraisal of the compatibility between reason and faith, but safeguards as well Tertullian's insistence that understanding of the things of God does not depend on sophisticated intellectual argument.

Aquinas' fundamental reason for asserting the compatibility between reason and faith is his confidence that 'the knowledge of naturally known principles is instilled into us by God, since God himself is the author of our nature'. He continues, 'Therefore those things which are received by faith from divine revelation cannot be contrary to our natural knowledge' (Aquinas, *Summa Contra Gentiles*, Book 1, ch. VII). Again, however, the theologians of the Protestant Reformation took a different view. While the goodness of God may well entail that we were created with a reliable knowledge of the truth, our intellects have been damaged by the fall so that our use of reason is now corrupted by self-interest, sinful desire, all kinds of prejudice and so on. An interesting comparison is to be noted here between this view and the more recent analyses of feminist thinkers and of postmodern theorists alike who have pointed out the degree to which human reasoning is shaped by patriarchal assumptions, cultural prejudices and other distorting influences that seriously inhibit the capacity of reason to attain unfettered access to the truth. While there is little agreement about the antidote to reason's malaise, Reformers like Luther and Calvin believed that sin's impairment of our reasoning power could be overcome only in virtue of the redemptive and reconciling work of God through which our whole lives, including our thinking, might be conformed to the truth that is revealed in Christ.

The competence of reason to give access to the truth continues to be disputed both within and beyond theology. The feminist and postmodern observations noted above, echoing the doubts of theologians throughout Christian history, have led many to reject the insistence of Enlightenment rationalism that reason was to be the final arbiter of all claims to truth. A more humble estimation of reason's prowess now seems to be appropriate. So far as theology is concerned, the seventeenth-century Calvinist theologian Francis Turretin (1623–87) expresses the matter well:

> The question is not whether reason has any use in theology. For we confess that its use is manifold both for illustration; for comparison; for inference; and for argumentation. But the question is simply whether it bears the relation of a principle and rule in whose scale the greatest mysteries of religion should be weighed, so that nothing should be held which is not agreeable to it, which is not founded upon and cannot be elicited from reason.
>
> (*The Institutes of Elenctic Theology*, 1, VIII.3)

For his own part, Turretin denies that reason should have the final say in matters of theology. He adopts the standard argument of the Reformers that reason is subject to the impairments of sin, but adds, among several other arguments, that 'it would be impious for a finite mind to circumscribe within narrow limits the infinite power of God'.

While the latter point especially would be accepted by most Christian theologians, it has been commonplace in modern Western culture to suppose that reason must be the final arbiter of all truth.

That is the view adopted by the 'New Atheists', among whom Richard Dawkins, Christopher Hitchens and Sam Harris have been especially prominent. While numerous debates have been held between religious believers and representatives of the New Atheism, the reasoned argument on both sides has failed to settle the central questions of whether or not God exists, whether belief in God is defeated by the existence of evil, whether religious faith yields more harm than good and so on. It has become very obvious that audiences listening to the debates and responding to them online assess the arguments on either side in light of the convictions with which they began. Very few are moved to change their minds by rational argumentation. There are factors other than the exercise of reason that seem to have a profound effect on what people profess to believe or disbelieve. As the French mathematician Blaise Pascal (1623–62) once put it, 'the heart has its reasons that reason knows nothing of' (Pascal, *Pensées*, iv.277) That observation alone gives cause to doubt that human reason has the competence the New Atheists claim for it. They might claim that human beings are inexplicably obstinate in the face of rational argumentation, but who is to say on which side of the theist/atheist debate the alleged obstinacy or the most coherent reasons lie? Reason cannot settle that question either, which lends weight to the suggestion made frequently in Christian theology that reason can be a servant but not the master of humanity's search for truth. It cannot claim to be the final arbiter in the questions that most deeply concern the nature and purpose of human life and of God's involvement in it.

EXPERIENCE

The suggestion put forward in the 'Age of Reason' that all questions of truth should be settled through rational deliberation met with considerable resistance in the movement known as Romanticism. Romantic poets, artists, musicians and theologians protested against what they perceived to be the reductive rationalism of scientific explanation and proposed that the truth of things is fully revealed only as we attend as well to aesthetic experience, emotion and a wisdom that goes beyond cold, hard rationalism. There is more to life and to the essential nature of things than reason and science can discover on their own. The Romantics urged us to attend not only to what was rational, but also to our feelings, our emotions, our imaginations, our sensitivity to the truth and order and beauty of things that couldn't be nailed down and measured and subjected to scientific experimentation. One should attend, in other words, not only to the mind, but also to the heart.

That aesthetic sensibility, it was argued, also gave us an inkling of God. The Romantics commonly argued that God could be discovered through the contemplation of nature, by being alert to the creative spirit that lies behind all things. Thus, for example, William Wordsworth (1770–1850) writes,

> And I have felt
> A presence that disturbs me with the joy
> Of elevated thoughts; a sense sublime
> Of something far more deeply interfused,
> Whose dwelling is the light of setting suns,
> And the round ocean and the living air,
> And the blue sky and the mind of Man
> A motion and a spirit, that impels
> All thinking things, all objects of all thoughts
> And rolls through all things.
>
>   ('Lines Composed a Few Miles Above Tintern Abbey')

Wordsworth was probably a pantheist, that is, someone who identified God with nature itself, but he illustrates nevertheless the Romantic conviction that the truth of things is to be discerned through aesthetic sensibility. The poets were likened by some to priests who mediated the things of God. John Keble, for instance, an Oxford scholar writing in 1844, dedicated his Lectures on Poetry to Wordsworth and wrote:

> TO WILLIAM WORDSWORTH
> TRUE PHILOSOPHER AND INSPIRED POET
> WHO BY THE SPECIAL GIFT AND CALLING OF ALMIGHTY GOD
> WHETHER HE SANG OF MAN OR OF NATURE
> FAILED NOT TO LIFT UP MEN'S HEARTS TO HOLY THINGS
> NOR EVER CEASED TO CHAMPION THE CAUSE
> OF THE POOR AND SIMPLE
> AND SO IN PERILOUS TIMES WAS RAISED UP

TO BE A CHIEF MINISTER
NOT ONLY OF SWEETEST POETRY
BUT ALSO OF HIGH AND SACRED TRUTH ...
(cited in Prickett, *Romanticism and Religion*, 92–96)

No longer the scientific rationalists, but the Romantic poets, musicians and artists were here supposed to be the ministers of high and sacred truth, providing a basis upon which we could speak of God.

Among theologians, the Romantic spirit reached its high point in the great German theologian Friedrich Schleiermacher (1768–1834). Schleiermacher contended that God is discovered as the reality underlying the religious experience of all human beings. It is through contemplation of one's own being that one becomes aware of God. Whereas Wordsworth claimed to discern through the contemplation of nature a 'spirit that rolls through all things', Schleiermacher considered that God is known through contemplation of our own existence, and most especially through the recognition that we are not the cause of our own being. We are fundamentally dependent upon some Other who is the source and sustainer of our being. Recognition of this 'absolute dependence' upon an 'Other' amounts, Schleiermacher says, to a consciousness of God. It is important to recognise that Schleiermacher's claim that we are dependent creatures is not a rational deduction akin to the cosmological argument for belief in God. The sense of dependence is better described as a feeling. We *sense* ourselves to be dependent. The experience of God involves warmth, affection and personal involvement. This experience, furthermore, is both fundamental to what it means to be human and the basis of all theological enquiry. While the development of Schleiermacher's theology involves rigorous and sophisticated intellectual enquiry, the foundation upon which it is developed is an experience that is readily accessible to all.

Schleiermacher is the forerunner of a conviction that has become widespread in contemporary Western culture, namely that theological and religious claims are credible only when they are grounded somehow in the individual's own experience. Two important examples of this appear in the form of feminist theology and liberation theology. Feminist theology is premised on the salutary observation that the way most societies have organised and interpreted the world is based on male experience and male perceptions of reality. Christian theology too has been prone to, and is, some would say, profoundly distorted by this male bias. This bias has been deeply damaging to women and has led to their oppression and marginalisation in the church. The refusal until relatively recently to ordain women, and then only in some churches, is one of the most obvious examples of this marginalisation, but it manifests itself in many ways throughout the church and in the church's theology. In light of this reality, feminist theology sets out to develop a theology that is based upon the experience and perceptions of women. One of the pioneers of feminist theology was the American scholar Mary Daly (1928–2010). Daly eventually came to the conclusion that Christian faith was irredeemably patriarchal and so ought to be rejected by women. Accordingly, Daly and others have left the Christian faith and in some cases have developed a theology or a spirituality that is described as post-Christian. Other feminist theologians have remained within the church, however, and have sought to reform the church and Christian theology from within. No single account of the approach taken by feminist theologians can adequately describe the rich variety of their contributions to contemporary theology, but they are united by the conviction that the experience and insights of women need to be given much more weight in the enterprise of theological enquiry.

A second widely influential movement in modern theology that draws heavily upon experience is liberation theology. Liberation theology was first developed in Latin America and was premised on the conviction that the experience of the poor and the oppressed yields radically different perceptions of the nature of the Christian gospel and, indeed, of the nature and purposes of God, than those typically found among rich Christians in the West. Those whose lives are dominated by the harsh realities of poverty and oppression hear Jesus' proclamation of good news to the poor and liberty to the captives as the fundamental message of the gospel and, in contrast with Western Christians who have tended to spiritualise the message of salvation, the poor see the promise of salvation in very concrete social, economic and political terms. Salvation for them, while certainly including a spiritual dimension, has to do as well with liberation from the oppressive social, political and economic systems that keep them in poverty and deny to them the dignity and freedom that the gospel promises. The experience of poverty and oppression led liberation theologians like Gustavo Gutiérrez to perceive in the biblical account of God's purposes a 'preferential option for the poor'. Put simply, Gutiérrez and others who worked with him in the slums of Latin America saw that again and again in the Bible, God sides with the oppressed and seeks to liberate them from the various forms their oppression takes. It was their own experience of poverty and oppression that drew their attention to this prominent feature of the biblical narrative so often overlooked by those who have no experience of such things.

The insights of feminist and liberation theologians reveal the positive impact that experience can have on theology, but there are also pitfalls in the appeal to experience that should be acknowledged. The pitfalls are evident in the very critique that feminist and liberation theologians have levelled against the theological tradition that has been dominated by the perceptions and experience of white, Western males. That limitation gives rise to substantial blind-spots and has yielded serious distortions in the church's theology and practice. That reality should dissuade us from making any individual's experience, or the experience of any particular group of people, absolutely authoritative. Claims based on one's own experience should be offered with a degree of humility and with recognition that they will likely stand in need of modification and correction by the testimony of others. That principle finds expression in the apostle Paul's advice to the church in Corinth concerning the essential contribution of all parts of the 'body' to the well-being of the church (see 1 Corinthians 12:12–31). In terms of theological enquiry, Paul's principle indicates that those who undertake the task of Christian theology should understand themselves to be involved in a shared endeavour that includes not only their own church or Christian tradition but a community that spans many generations and many locations. Theologians must attend to the voices of Christians who are vastly different from themselves in terms of ethnicity, culture, language, heritage, gender, socio-economic status and so on. Equally, however, they must attend to the voices of those who have gone before them in the course of Christianity's long history and whose insight into the nature of the gospel can help individual theologians of a particular cultural context to see beyond the horizons of their own limited interests and concerns.

A further limitation upon the authority of appeals to experience is the reality of human sin. We human beings are inclined to perceive things and make judgements about what is going on in the world with a certain degree of self-interest. That can blind us to the interests of others, colour our perceptions of things and lead us to draw conclusions that are limited at best and seriously distorted and damaging at their worst. Theologians should be wary, therefore, of placing too much weight on their own perceptions, feelings and judgements, and acknowledge the need for correction through exposure to insights that are not their own. More particularly, theologians, along with all who seek understanding of the nature of reality, must acknowledge their need for correction and transformation through exposure to the reality with which they are concerned. In the case of theology, of course, that reality is God. That is why, however much theologians may draw upon tradition, reason and experience, the proper place to begin theology is with prayer. Theologians must humbly submit themselves again and again to the searching light of God's own Word present among us in the person of Jesus Christ and sounded again in the biblical witness. That is the point at which theology begins and the point to which it must constantly return.

FURTHER READING

There is a wide range of views on the nature and methods of Christian theology. Samples of that breadth are presented in *The Practice of Theology: A Reader*, edited by Colin E. Gunton, Stephen R. Holmes and Murray A. Rae (London: SCM Press, 2001). See also Trevor Hart, *Faith Thinking, The Dynamics of Christian Theology* (London: SPCK, 1995); *The Cambridge Companion to Feminist Theology*, edited by Susan Frank Parsons (Cambridge: Cambridge University Press, 2002); *An Introduction to Third World Theologies*, edited by John Parratt (Cambridge: Cambridge University Press, 2004); and *Introducing Liberation Theology* by Leonardo Boff and Clodovis Boff (Tunbridge Wells, UK: Burns and Oates, 1987).

2

CREATION AND COVENANT

As is well known, the Bible begins with an account of the world's creation. It begins with the claim that all things have their origin in the creative agency of God and are brought into being at God's behest. One of the most striking features of the account of creation given in Genesis 1 is that the world is well ordered. Light is distinguished from darkness, and a pattern is established whereby night follows day in a regular and consistent order. The sun, the moon and the stars are set in the heavens so that they may provide light sufficient to what is required by day and by night, and to give length to the days and the years and the seasons. Dry land is separated from the sea, and a space is opened up between the earth and the sky so that the living creatures have a place to dwell. The dry land thus created is a suitable place for vegetation, for plants bearing seed and trees bearing fruit. The earth, the sea and the sky provide places of habitation for the vast array of living creatures, including human beings, who are said to be made in God's image and who are given a particular role as stewards of all that God has made. The world is a suitable place for the flourishing of all living things and, according to the story in Genesis 1, God saw that it was good.

WHAT KIND OF LITERATURE DO WE FIND IN GENESIS?

We will come in due course to say something of the disorder and the evil that afflicts the world, but the Bible's confession of God's *good* ordering of things 'in the beginning' is an enormously important affirmation with wide-ranging implications. Before exploring this affirmation further, however, we need to consider what kind of literature we are dealing with in Genesis 1. Some Christians regard the account of creation in Genesis 1 as something akin to an historical or even a scientific report. They treat it as an account of what an observer might have seen had he or she been there during the seven-day period in which the world is said to have been brought into being. The imagined observer of creation would thus have seen all the plants of the earth spring forth within a single day, and a couple of days later all the animals, birds and fish would have appeared, and so on. This approach is often described as a literal reading of Genesis 1. As is well known, however, such an approach brings the reader of Scripture into conflict with the findings of modern science, especially, of course, with the widespread scientific consensus that life on earth came about through a process of evolution taking millions of years. While the theory of evolution leaves some things unexplained, and while there are gaps in the evolutionary record that can be filled at this stage only by well-founded conjecture, the overwhelming majority of scientists agree that there is abundant evidence to confirm the view that life emerged on earth through the evolutionary development of living creatures. Those who maintain a literal reading of Genesis 1 therefore find themselves having to deny, or having to find some other explanation for, the vast body of evidence in favour of evolution.

For many Christians, however, the assumption that one must choose between the biblical record and the findings of modern science is misguided, at least in this case. The supposed conflict arises only, they suggest, from a failure to appreciate the genre of the Genesis text. The various texts of the Bible are not all of the same kind. They include prayers, historical narratives, prophecies, parables, laments, legal codes and so on. When reading a particular text, therefore, it is important to pay attention to what kind of text it is. When we read the story of the prodigal son in Luke 15, for example, we recognise that this is not an historical report. It would not make sense for the reader to visit modern-day Israel so as to locate the farm from which the young man departed and to which he eventually made his way home. The story is clearly recognisable as a parable; it is not a literal account of some series of historical events. Recognition of that fact, however, does not undermine the profound theological importance of the parable or the truth it reveals about human beings and about God's dealings with us. The genre of parable turns out to be, in this instance, a profound and very effective means of truth-telling. The truth revealed through the parable of the prodigal son is not at all dependent upon our being able to locate the farm, or trace the descendants of the family spoken of in the parable. Indeed, most readers would recognise that any effort to do so would be a very unfortunate way of missing the point.

Returning to Genesis 1, many Christians regard the story of creation found there as the kind of literature that is much more like a parable than an historical or scientific report. The same observations about the truth of the story as were noted above with respect to the parable of the prodigal son apply here as well. Recognition of Genesis 1 as a kind of parable does not undermine in any way the profound truth to which it testifies. Nor does it threaten the authority of the Bible. The truth to which Genesis 1 testifies and its authority as the Word of God remains intact, just as the truth and authority of Jesus' parables is not undermined by the fact that they are not historical narratives.

THE ORDER OF CREATION

To what, then, does Genesis 1 testify? Well, it testifies, as we have noted, to the good ordering of creation. The world is not a chaotic or meaningless series of random and unintelligible events. Rather, it exhibits a high degree of coherence, consistency and intelligibility. The story of creation in Genesis 1 affirms that this good ordering of things is no accident but has been arranged by God in order to bring about his purposes. Although some scientists tell us that they are atheists and so contend that no God was involved in establishing the order and intelligibility of the cosmos, that is their own personal judgement and cannot be regarded as a finding of science. By contrast, there are numerous scientists who accept the findings of modern science and find no difficulty in upholding the theological claim of Genesis 1 that the fine-tuning of the cosmos to support and nourish life on earth is attributable to the work of God. It is important to note here that the natural sciences themselves depend upon the universe being well ordered and intelligible in just the way that

Genesis 1 affirms. If there were no order to the cosmos, if all that happens in the world were just a series of haphazard and unconnected events, then science could not function. There would be no 'laws' governing the behaviour of nature, no predictability in the things that happen and thus no possibility of making sense of anything that happens. Thus science, and indeed all of human life, depends upon this basic affirmation of the Genesis text being true, namely that the world has a high level of order and intelligibility. The more science can reveal of this order and intelligibility, the more it confirms the basic insight of the biblical text. The point in dispute between the atheist and the believer is whether the order and intelligibility of the universe has a cause outside itself. Did it come to be by accident or is it the fruit of God's creative work?

CREATION OUT OF NOTHING

Although it is not stated explicitly in the accounts of creation provided in the book of Genesis or elsewhere in the Bible, Christian theologians have commonly argued that the world is created by God *ex nihilo*, meaning 'out of nothing'. The theologians of the early church thus distanced themselves from the Greek notion that matter is eternal, and from the Gnostic idea that the things of this world emanate from the divine being. The doctrine of *creatio ex nihilo* affirms, simply, that matter is not eternal; it has not always existed but has a beginning. God created matter rather than fabricating a world out of materials that were already lying about in space. It is interesting to note that this theological view was resisted by science until the mid-twentieth century, when the so-called 'Big Bang Theory' emerged as the most likely explanation of the beginning of the universe. The theologians of the early church did not insist that the world was created out of nothing for scientific reasons, however, but for theological reasons. They argued that if God were not the sole creator of all that exists, then God's sovereignty would be compromised. God would have to deal with entities for which he is not responsible and which, to some degree at least, lie outside his control. The biblical affirmation of the absolute sovereignty of God seemed to demand that all things come to be and have their existence in virtue of God's sovereign and creative power. Accordingly, theologians have commonly affirmed that nothing exists prior to or apart from God's creative agency. The world is created *ex nihilo*. The doctrine of creation out of nothing has been contested by some contemporary theologians, particularly within 'process theology' and some forms of feminist theology. A brief account of these objections can be found in David Fergusson's discussion of creation in *The Oxford Handbook of Systematic Theology*.

> Process theology is a form of theology developed especially in the twentieth century in which the being of God is thought to be bound up with the unfolding of time and history. Drawing heavily upon the philosophy of Alfred North Whitehead, two of its leading proponents have been Charles Hartshorne and John B. Cobb Jr.

THE 'TELOS' OF CREATION

A further implication of the idea that the world was created out of nothing is that it has some purpose. The world is intended, rather than just happens to be. The Greek word commonly used in this connection is *telos*, which means 'end' or 'purpose'. The doctrine of *creatio ex nihilo* is taken to imply that God creates for some reason. The creation is a project of some sort, through which God seeks to achieve some purpose. That conviction makes a great deal of difference to how we understand human history. It can no longer be thought of as a series of random events, as simply 'one damn thing after another', as Henry Ford once put it, but as a project of God that is directed towards some purpose. We will return to this theme later in the chapter. First, however, there is more to be said about the nature of the God who is the creator of all things.

THE TRIUNE CREATOR

We are told, in Genesis 1, that when God first created the heavens and the earth, 'the earth was a formless void and darkness covered the face of the deep … ' (Genesis 1:2). Matter has been formed but it has not yet been given order, and, on account of the darkness, it is not yet intelligible. But then we read that a wind from God swept over the face of the waters, and God said, 'Let there be light'.

Although the point will almost certainly be lost on those who hear this story for the first time, those more familiar with the way the biblical story unfolds will hear overtones in these two affirmations that are enormously significant for Christian theology. They will hear overtones, first of all, in the phrase 'a wind from God'. The Hebrew word translated here as 'wind' is *ruach*. The word can also be translated – and often is elsewhere in the Bible – as breath or spirit. The presence of a breath or spirit from God is a condition leading to the formation of living things. This idea that life depends upon the gift of God's breath or spirit is evident a few verses later when in Genesis 2:7 we read that 'the Lord God formed man from the dust of the ground and breathed into his nostrils the breath of life: and the man became a living being'. The theme recurs often in the Bible. In Psalm 104, for instance, the Psalmist, speaking of the myriad creatures on the earth, writes: ' ... when you take away their breath, they die and return to their dust. When you send forth your spirit, they are created: and you renew the face of the ground' (Psalm 104:29–30). The same idea is found in Job 34:14–15: 'If he [God] should take back his spirit to himself and gather to himself his breath, all flesh would perish together, and all mortals return to dust.' Those familiar with these biblical texts will hear the overtones in Genesis 1:2. The wind or the spirit of God, sweeping over the face of the waters, prefigures the emergence of life. The presence of God's *ruach* is a condition without which life could not exist.

Elsewhere in the Old Testament the term *ruach* is used to name that which is essential to personal being. In Psalm 31:5, for example, 'Into your hand, I commit my spirit', or Psalm 32:2, 'Blessed are those ... in whose spirit there is no deceit', the term refers to the distinctively personal character and essential identity of human beings. In like manner, reference to the Spirit of God in the Old Testament increasingly indicates God's personal presence, while in the New Testament the Spirit takes on a personal character distinct from and yet intimately bound up with the person of God the Father and the person of the Son, Jesus Christ. We will say more of this in chapter three. At the time that Genesis 1:2 was written, the full resonance of the term *ruach* or spirit was, undoubtedly, yet to be heard, but Christians reading now of the wind or spirit of God that swept over the face of the waters and gives life to the creation are likely to recognise that *ruach* as the same Spirit who is revealed through Christ, at Pentecost, and in the ongoing life of the church in our own day.

Christians are likely to hear overtones too in the phrase 'God said, let there be light' (Genesis 1:3). The light emerges and things become visible, and intelligible, through the utterance of God's Word. This utterance becomes a repeating pattern. On each of the remaining days of creation recounted in Genesis 1, God's Word is the creative agency through which the world is given order and the succession of living things comes to be. The overtones are sounded here, not least because of the opening verses of John's gospel: 'In the beginning was the Word, and the Word was with God, and the Word was God. He was in the beginning with God. All things came into being through Him … ' (John 1:1–3). As happened with the Spirit of God, so now the Word is recognised as personal in character. Indeed, John's gospel is soon to make the point very clear: 'And the Word became flesh and lived among us, and we have seen his glory, the glory as of a father's only son, full of grace and truth' (John 1:14). These are words from the prologue of John's gospel, the prologue to John's account of Jesus, the beloved Son of God, who takes on our human flesh yet is in person the very Word of God.

The movement by which the eternal Word of God 'becomes flesh' is known as the incarnation.

Whoever it was who first wrote the story of creation in Genesis 1 will not have understood what he wrote in terms of the later Christian convictions that the spirit present in creation is the same Spirit who was poured out upon the church at Pentecost, and that the Word through which creation was called into being is the same Word who is made flesh in Jesus, but there is a coherence between the Genesis account and what was later discovered to be true of God. This coherence has led Christians to affirm that it is none other than the Triune God, Father, Son and Spirit, who made all things and who has declared that they are good.

The affirmation that the world was created by the Triune God rules out a deistic conception of God's relation to the creation.

Deism is the belief that God created the world but then withdraws from it and leaves it to run according to the 'laws of nature' that God established. According to the deistic view, God does not intervene in the course of the world's history. God is uninvolved in the creation except as the one who brought it into being and determined the laws by which it operates. This is not a Christian view, for Christian faith affirms that God is present in the midst of history through his Word and Spirit. God is at work among us sustaining the creation through his life-giving Spirit, redeeming the creation following humanity's fateful decision to go its way in defiance of God's good purposes, and perfecting creation by enabling it to become in the end what God intends it to be. The second-century theologian Irenaeus of Lyon spoke of God's continuing involvement in creation by referring to the Son and Spirit as the 'two hands' of God (see Irenaeus, *Against Heresies*, Book IV, Preface, 4). God is involved in the course of history, Irenaeus affirmed, and is bringing about his purpose through his Spirit and his Word.

DOMINION

A further feature of the creation account in Genesis 1 is that God enlists human participation in the project of creation. Human beings are not mere puppets; nor are they mere bystanders as the drama of God's purposes is worked out. Rather, human beings are appointed to a particular role in the created order. They are instructed to 'have dominion' over every living thing (Genesis 1:28). This is an especially salutary instruction given our growing awareness of the destructive effects of humanity's exploitation of nature. In a widely read article written in 1967 and titled 'The Historical Roots of Our Ecologic Crisis', Lynn White Jr. argued that the biblical instruction to have dominion over the earth is the root cause of our present environmental crisis. According to White, this biblical injunction gives license to human beings to exploit nature for their own ends and has led Christians to believe that the natural world exists only to serve human needs or desires. While White's argument has been widely contested both in terms of its historical accuracy and because of its questionable interpretation of the Genesis text, his article has highlighted the need for serious theological reflection in the context of contemporary environmental concerns.

There can be no escaping the biblical insistence that human beings have been given dominion over all living creatures – the Hebrew word translated as 'dominion' is *radah* – but what does dominion or *radah* mean in this context? *Radah* certainly does mean to rule over or have dominion. Likewise, the Latin root of the word 'dominion', namely *domini*, can be translated as lord, and so, having dominion can mean to exercise lordship. It is at this point, however, that a theological understanding of the term becomes crucial. Lordship, as exercised by Jesus, by the one whom Christians confess to be the true Lord, takes the form of compassionate and humble service. The nature of his Lordship is revealed in his taking a towel and washing his disciples' feet; it is revealed in his refusal to seize political power or to take up the sword in pursuit of his cause; it is revealed, above all, in the giving up of his own life for the sake of the world. Self-sacrifice, compassion and service are the marks of dominion when exercised by the one who truly deserves to be called Lord. This Christological interpretation of what Lordship means commends to us a rather different account of human dominion than has been suggested by Lynn White. Exploitation and domination have no part in Jesus' exercise of dominion. This interpretation is consistent too with the use of the word *radah* in Psalm 72. In a prayer for the king, the Psalmist writes, 'May he have dominion [*radah*] from sea to sea, and from the River to the ends of the earth' (Psalm 72:8). The Psalmist continues, 'For he delivers the needy when they call, the poor and those who have no helper. He has pity on the weak and the needy, and saves the lives of the needy. From oppression and violence he redeems their life; and precious is their blood in his sight' (Psalm 72:12–14). The dominion exercised here is remarkably like the dominion exercised by Christ and gives further guidance on how those given dominion in Genesis 1:28 ought to understand their task.

Picking up this idea of compassionate care for the creation, many have employed the word 'stewardship' in describing the responsibility assigned to humanity in the Genesis story. Whatever language we are to use, the biblical account of creation encourages respect for the goodness of God's creation and suggests that because the earth's goodness is received as a blessing from God's hand we ought to hand it on, still as a blessing, to those who will come after us.

DIVINE PURPOSE

Although science and theology can agree that the cosmos is endowed with a high level of order and intelligibility, Christian theology claims further that the world is also invested with a purpose. Its order and its goodness did not come about by accident but are intended. This is a statement of faith. It is a faith that is confirmed, as we shall discuss further in subsequent chapters, by the life, death and resurrection of Jesus, but it arises first in the context of God's call upon Israel to be his people and his promise that the divine blessing will be extended through Israel to all the families of the earth. The goodness of all that God has made consists, accordingly, in the suitability of creation for the bringing about of God's purposes. While this may seem to be a straightforward and relatively uncontroversial theological claim, it is one that has had to be defended again and again against two contrasting views.

The first such opposing view was that held by the Greek or Hellenistic culture that dominated the environment in which Christianity emerged. In classical Greek thought the material world, the *cosmos aisthetos*, or world of appearances, was regarded as of lesser value than the *cosmos noetos*, the intelligible or eternal world that lay beyond the merely material. This was the world of the forms, as the Greek philosopher Plato put it, the world of eternal and pure ideas. The earth we inhabit, by contrast, contains in its material objects only a vast array of imperfect and shadowy reflections of the ideal form of things. Because matter is subject to constant change and decay, it is thought to be inherently unstable and imperfect and cannot reveal the true nature of things. The truth can be learned only by setting aside the distractions of material life and by exercising our reason to attain knowledge of the eternal world of the forms. To declare in a culture such as this that the material world is good appeared to be utter foolishness. The proclamation in John 1:14 that the eternal Word of God had become flesh would have appeared to be equally absurd. It was simply inconceivable to the Greek way of thinking that the eternal truth of things and the working out of the divine purpose might be revealed in and through the material realities of this world. Surely we ought to look to a world beyond this one in order to discern the true reality and purposes of God. This assumption became in the early church a considerable obstacle to the spread of the gospel.

Plato's theory of the forms has been very influential in Western thought. The form of a thing is its true essence and exists not as a concrete material reality but as an abstract idea. According to Plato, we do not discover the essence of things by observing their occurrence in the material world, but by rational contemplation of the abstract idea that is expressed only imperfectly in particular instances of the thing. The study of the material world, accordingly, is considered by Plato to be an unreliable means of learning the truth of things.

Acceptance of this gospel, acceptance of the news that God had come among us in Jesus, required a radical transformation of one's whole way of seeing things. The apostle Paul called this transformation *metanoia*. *Metanoia* combines the two Greek words *meta* (transform) and *nous* (mind) and so means conversion, or a radical transformation of one's mind. Not surprisingly, therefore, a gospel that required such a transformation met with considerable resistance by people determined to retain their customary ways of thinking about the world. This resistance was most obvious in a collection of ideas known as Gnosticism. Gnostic thinkers like Valentinus (*c*.100–*c*.160) and Basilides (*c*.100–*c*.139) appear, so far as we can tell through the writings of their opponents, particularly Irenaeus, to have promoted an elaborate cosmology in which the material world was regarded as inferior to the spiritual world and an impediment to salvation. The material world was thought to have been created not by the supreme God but by an inferior god, or demiurge, whose bungling and inept creativity accounts for the world's imperfection and evil. Within this scheme, the mission of Christ is to free human beings from the captivity of material existence and to lead them into a higher form of spiritual existence. We need not consider these Gnostic ideas any further here, except to reiterate their incompatibility both with the view expressed in Genesis that God has declared his creation to be good and with the conviction of the New Testament writers that in Jesus God has become fully participant in the realities of our material existence.

> Although the authenticity of the quote is disputed, the story goes that in response to Emperor Napoleon's comment that 'You have written this huge book on the system of the world without once mentioning the author of the universe', Laplace responded, 'Sir, I had no need of that hypothesis.'

A second form of resistance to the idea that the goodness of creation consists in its suitability for the bringing about of God's purposes is more commonly found in our own age and predominantly in Western culture. The resistance in this case is not directed against the idea that the world has a certain goodness or value, but against the suggestion that there is a divine purpose being worked out through the course of the world's history. There is a strong tendency in Western culture today to regard the world as self-contained and self-explanatory. As it is alleged to have been put by the French astronomer and mathematician Pierre-Simon Laplace, many Westerners apparently now think that 'we have no need of the God hypothesis' in order to account for or make sense of what goes on in the world. Perhaps more common still, in Western culture at least, is the view that there is ultimately no meaning in human existence save what we bestow upon it ourselves. We live, we die, that's it! This view is expressed in a despairing speech delivered by William Shakespeare's Macbeth.

> To-morrow, and to-morrow, and to-morrow,
> Creeps in this petty pace from day to day,
> To the last syllable of recorded time;
> And all our yesterdays have lighted fools
> The way to dusty death. Out, out, brief candle!
> Life's but a walking shadow; a poor player,
> That struts and frets his hour upon the stage,
> And then is heard no more. It is a tale
> Told by an idiot, full of sound and fury,
> Signifying nothing.
>
> (Shakespeare, *Macbeth*, Act V, Scene V)

The Christian doctrine of creation offers an alternative to this despairing view, for it holds that the world exists in consequence of God's intent that there should be something other than himself. A particular feature of God's intent is that there should be persons who are called to live in communion with him.

HUMANITY MADE IN GOD'S IMAGE

That communion lies at the heart of God's creative purposes is indicated to begin with by the biblical affirmation that human beings are made in God's image (Genesis 1:26–27). This is not said of other creatures and so, for all that human beings share much with other animals, a fact evident in our genetic makeup, there is nevertheless something distinctive about human beings. Uniquely among the creatures that God has made, human beings are said to be made in God's image. But what does this mean? The Bible itself does not give a clear answer to this question. For much of Christian history, it has been argued that we are distinguished most clearly from other creatures by our capacity for rational thought. It has been argued, therefore, that the image of God refers to our capacity to reason. Despite the prevalence of this view in theological tradition, however, the Bible provides little support for it. That is just as well, for if the image of God in us were to be identified with our capacity for rational thought, then we should have to doubt whether new-born infants, or those whose minds have deteriorated in old age, or those suffering from mental illness or impairment could still be said to bear the image of God. The same two objections, namely a lack of biblical support and problematic ethical implications, apply to the rival theory that the image of God refers to our moral capacity. More biblical support can be claimed for the idea that the image consists in our being given dominion over the earth. The instruction of God to be fruitful and multiply and to have dominion over the earth follows in Genesis 1:28 immediately after the claim that human beings are made in God's image, thus leading some commentators to suggest that verse 28 interprets what it means to be made in God's image.

Recent theological opinion, however, has tended towards the view that the image of God is to be understood not so much in terms of some human capacity or other but in terms of our correspondence to God. That is, our identity as human beings is established, safeguarded and perfected by virtue of the fact that God loves us, addresses us and calls us to live in relationship with him. Whatever our rational or moral capacity, and however well or however poorly we have exercised those capacities, our correspondence to God remains fundamental to our identity. We were made to live in relationship with God and are his beloved sons and daughters come what may. It is in this, arguably, that our distinctive humanity consists. This relational conception of human being extends horizontally to our fellow human beings. Our relationships with others are not secondary to who we are but are an essential feature of what it is to be human. This is indicated perhaps by the statement in Genesis 1:27 that 'God created humankind in his image, in the image of God he created them; male and female he created them.' We are made in correspondence with one another at the human level as well. A second account of the creation of humankind in Genesis 2 likewise places a great deal of emphasis upon humanity's existence in relationship. Following the creation of man, God says, 'It is not good that the man should be alone' (Genesis 2:18). God proceeds therefore to find a companion for the man, a search that culminates in the creation of a woman (Genesis 2:22–23). According to this biblical view of our relational nature, it is a mistake to conceive of ourselves in individualistic terms. We are not isolated or self-contained individuals who may choose to enter into relations with others or not. Rather, the relations in which we find ourselves, with God and with neighbour, are constitutive of our identity as human beings.

Biblical support for this conception of the image of God comes in the form of Paul's affirmation that Christ is the true image of God. In 2 Corinthians 4:4, Paul refers to the 'glory of Christ who is the image (*eikon*) of God', while Colossians 1:15 speaks of Christ as 'the image (*eikon*) of the invisible God, the first-born of all creation'. It seems unlikely that Paul is here referring to Christ's rational powers or to his moral capacity. What is most distinctive about Christ's humanity is the way it is ordered to God. Christ's whole life is shaped by the love that binds him to God and that flows without restraint to his fellow human beings. In the same way, though less clearly, for in us the image of God has been obscured by sin, our humanity is constituted by the relationship of love for which we were made and that God upholds even when we do our worst. As we will explore further in chapter five, the importance of relationship with God and with neighbour lies behind the biblical account of sin as the rupturing of relationship, and of salvation as the restoration of right relationship.

COVENANT

Right relationship with God and with neighbour could lay claim to being the central theme of the Bible. We have considered briefly already God's good ordering of creation. God's creative ordering of the cosmos involved setting things in right relation; the sea is distinguished from the dry land, the night is set in appropriate relation to the day and so on. We have noted as well the relationality of human beings to one another and to God. Although our being made in God's image establishes human beings as creatures who exist in a very particular relation to God, the principle of right relationship across the whole creation occurs again and again in the Bible. In Genesis 9, for instance, following the great flood, God is said to establish a covenant, first of all, with Noah and his descendants (Genesis 9:9) but extending as well to 'every living creature' (Genesis 9:10, 12, 15) and indeed to the whole earth (Genesis 9:13). The covenant takes the form of a promise in which one party binds him- or herself to another. In the case of God's covenant with Noah, God binds himself to his creatures by promising that he will never again 'cut off' all flesh by the waters of a flood. James Torrance explains that a covenant is 'a promise binding two people or two parties to love one another *unconditionally*' (see Torrance, 'Covenant or Contract?', p. 54). The unconditional nature of a covenant distinguishes it from a contract. A covenant is not conditional upon the other party fulfilling some condition or conditions. It is a promise that is to be honoured, come what may. When, a little later in the biblical story, God establishes a covenant with Israel, saying, 'I will take you as my people and I will be your God' (Exodus 6:7, cf. Leviticus 26:12; Jeremiah 30:22), it becomes clear that God binds himself to the people of Israel and will remain committed to them even in the face of Israel's unfaithfulness (see, e.g., Leviticus 26:44–45). The story of the Bible, then, is the story of the working out of this relationship that is initiated with Israel but ultimately extends to the whole creation.

The centrality to the biblical story of this covenantal relationship between God and his creatures led the great twentieth-century theologian Karl Barth (1886–1968) to propose that the covenant relationality to be worked out between God and his creatures is the very reason for creation in the first place. 'What God created when He created the world and man', Barth writes, 'was not just any place, but that which was foreordained for the establishment and the history of the covenant, nor just any subject, but that which was to become God's partner in this history … ' (Barth, *Church Dogmatics*, IV.2, p. 231). I suggested earlier that one of the implications of the idea that the world was created *ex nihilo*, out of nothing, is that the world is *intended*. It is created for some purpose. Barth here suggests, following the biblical story, that the world exists for the sake of the covenant, for the sake, that is, of the relationship that God seeks with his creatures. But why should God do this? The most satisfactory answer that Christian theology can give to this question is that God creates something other than himself because God is love. Creation is brought into being through the outflowing of God's love. God does not desire to be alone but seeks to live in relationship with one whom he creates as his partner. Creation, Barth says, is 'the realisation of the *divine* intention of love' (Barth, *Church Dogmatics*, IV.2, p. 96). This entails, clearly, that

> The creature is not self-existent. It has not assumed its nature and existence of itself or given it to itself. It did not come into being by itself. It does not consist by itself. It has to thank its creation and therefore its Creator for the fact that it came into being and is and will be. It is not the creature itself but its Creator who exists and thinks and speaks and cares for the creature. The creature is no more its own goal and purpose than its own ground and beginning.
>
> (Barth, *Church Dogmatics*, IV.2, p. 94)

Here again the relational identity of human being is made explicit. Human beings are not isolated individual entities existing independently of God and of other persons. To be a human being is to exist before God, and in relation with all that God has made. This is what authentic humanity consists in. To be human is to be created by God, to be addressed by God, to be elected by God as God's covenant partner and so to live in relation with all others to whom God gives life. Put otherwise, we are made to live in harmonious co-existence with God, with our neighbour and with all that God has made.

CREATION AND FALL

That human beings are made to live in relationship with God was a cause of wonder to the ancient writer of Psalm 8. Pondering the apparent insignificance of human beings in the vast expanse of the universe, the Psalmist wrote:

> When I look at your heavens, the work of your fingers,
> the moon and the stars that you have established;
> what are human beings that you are mindful of them,
> mortals, that you care for them?
> Yet you have made them a little lower than God,
> and crowned them with glory and honour.
> You have given them dominion over the works of your hands;
> you have put all things under their feet.
>
> (Psalm 8:3–6)

Stewardship of creation is one aspect of the covenant partnership to which humanity is called by God, but the more fundamental glory of humanity is found in the fact that human beings are created and cared for by God. Their glory is that they are loved by God and may in turn love him. It is the apprehension of this relationality, as it is disclosed most fully in Christ, that enables us to see also, however, the tragedy of humanity's determination to live for itself, according to its own ends, and in pursuit of its own selfish purposes.

The biblical account of creation and the appointing of humanity to live in relationship with God includes within it the tragedy of humanity's taking to itself the prerogative to determine the form of its own existence, to go its way apart from God. It is in the very nature of God's being for us as love that our being for God cannot be coerced. We can turn away. We can refuse the covenant relationality in which we were created. Even *that* freedom is bestowed upon us by God himself. We can decide against God. We can choose disobedience. God has not made it impossible for us to disobey, to choose the direction of our own life, and to go our way without him.

It is part of the error of sinfulness, however, that we imagine that self-determination and self-sufficiency are the means by which we may be truly human. The temptation offered to humanity by the serpent in Genesis 3 is 'to be like God'. The serpent laid down the possibility that humanity might see its own needs better than

God does, and satisfy those needs for itself. Ironically, however, God himself does not seek such self-sufficiency. God himself determines to be God, not in some isolated and non-relational individuality; rather, God is love. He determines to be God in loving relation, both in his own Triune being as Father, Son and Spirit, but also in his movement outward in creation through which humanity is given the scope and the freedom to be God's covenant partner. The human quest for individual self-subsistence and self-assertion is not godlike at all, but a rejection of the relationality in which God himself exists.

RELATIONAL BEING

Recognition of the relational being of God has prompted a great deal of interest in recent theological discussion. The Greek Orthodox theologian John Zizioulas (1931–) has argued, for example, that the relational understanding of the three persons of the Trinity that was developed in the early church led to a relational conception of what it is to be a human person. While some aspects of Zizioulas' analysis have been contested, few theologians would disagree that the individualistic conception of human personhood in which persons are supposed to be isolated and self-contained beings fails to do justice to the biblical understanding of human identity. Personal identity is irreducibly bound up with our relations with God and with one another. The individualistic conception of human personhood, by contrast, is an idea that has developed largely in Western culture. The Christian thinker and Roman senator Boethius (c.480–c.524), for example, described the person as 'an individual substance of a rational nature'. Relations with others played no part in the definition of the person. This idea would later gain traction in Western culture through thinkers such as Descartes who, in the development of his famous proposition 'I think, therefore I am', defined the human being simply as 'a thinking thing'.

These individualistic understandings of human identity are quite foreign to many non-Western cultures, including, for example, the cultures of Polynesian people in the South Pacific. It is inconceivable to Pacific Island and Māori people to think of their identity as persons apart from their relations to their family and to their village, in the case of Pacific Islanders, or to their tribe, in the case of Māori. Similarly, in African cultures, personal identity is typically conceived in relational terms. Peter Kasenene, a contemporary politician and former Professor of Comparative Religion in Uganda, explains in an article on 'Ethics in African Theology' that African peoples typically think about ethical questions in much more relational ways than Western people. Feminist theologians too have argued that individualistic and self-assertive conceptions of personal identity are a manifestation of human fallenness to which males are especially prone. Women are more inclined, it is suggested, to conceive of our humanity in relational terms.

TRUE HUMANITY

The relational account of human being offered by feminist theologians and by theologians from Africa and from the South Pacific fits well with the biblical story we have been following of God's creation of humankind in his image and with God's intention that human beings should live in communion with God and with one another. This relational conception of our existence is confirmed by the life that Jesus lives, by the life, that is, of the one whom Christian tradition confesses to be truly human, as well as truly divine. In Jesus Christ, rather than in the fallen humanity that we see all about us, we learn what it is to be truly human. We see human life guided and empowered by the Spirit and lived at all times in loving response to God the Father. Equally, the life of Jesus is at all times a consistent expression of his compassion for others. He lives for others, rather than for himself. This denial of self, however, should not be misunderstood. The 'self' that Jesus denies is not the true human self, but the self-interested, self-contained, self-absorbed humanity that is the essence of human sin. This is the self that Jesus calls us to set aside in taking up our cross and following him. Those who do so, Jesus further reveals, those who entrust their lives to him, do not lose their life but gain it (see Mark 8:35; Matthew 16:25). True human being, it turns out after all, is realised in that communion of love with God and with our neighbour that has been God's purpose for us from the beginning.

FURTHER READING

Helpful outlines of the doctrine of creation may be found in David Fergusson, 'Creation', in *The Oxford Handbook of Systematic Theology*, edited by John Webster, Kathryn Tanner and Iain Torrance (Oxford: Oxford University Press, 2007), 72–90. A more advanced but important recent treatment of creation is Colin Gunton's *The Triune Creator* (Edinburgh: Edinburgh University Press, 1998). On the care of creation, see R. J. Berry, ed., *The Care of Creation: Focussing Concern and Action* (Leicester: Inter-Varsity Press, 2000).

A good introduction to theological anthropology is offered in Kelly Kapic, 'Anthropology', in *Mapping Modern Theology: A Thematic and Historical Introduction*, edited by Kelly M. Kapic and Bruce L. McCormack (Grand Rapids, MI: Baker Academic, 2012), 121–48. Relational conceptions of personhood are fruitfully explored in Peter Kasenene, 'Ethics in African Theology', in *Doing Ethics in Context: South African Perspectives*, eds C. Villa-Vicencio and John de Gruchy (Maryknoll, NY: Orbis Books, 1994), 138–47, and in Virginia Held, 'Reason, Gender and Moral Theory', in *Ethics*, ed. Peter Singer (Oxford: Oxford University Press, 1994), 166–70. More adventurous readers might consider Karl Barth's discussion of humanity in Volume III.2 of his *Church Dogmatics*.

3

JESUS AND THE SPIRIT

In the preceding chapter we encountered the claim that God is at work in history. In the account of creation presented in Genesis 1, it is the movement of a wind or spirit from God that signals the first stirrings of creation, while the world is brought into being as God speaks his Word. In a second account of the creation of human beings, found in Genesis 2, it is said that 'the Lord God formed man from the dust of the ground, and breathed into his nostrils the breath of life; and the man became a living being' (Genesis 2:7). We observed as well that this work of Word and Spirit is understood by Christians, and by Jews too, to be a continuing reality in our world. God is involved not only at the beginning of creation but throughout history. God continues to be the giver and the sustainer of life, and is the one, so Christians believe, who will bring the creation to completion.

The central claim of the New Testament is that this work of God takes place most especially in and through the person of Jesus and through the guidance and enabling of the Spirit. In the opening verses of John's gospel, Jesus is spoken of as the Word made flesh. As his life unfolds, it becomes apparent that Jesus enjoys a close relationship with the Spirit. The same Word and Spirit spoken of in the Old Testament continue the work of God through the story told in the New.

Jesus of Nazareth was, of course, a very controversial figure. His life and his teaching provoked outrage amongst the religious authorities of his day and caused enough friction for the political authorities to order his execution by the most brutal means available. The writers of the New Testament, however, speak on behalf of another group. They speak for those who became convinced that through their encounters with Jesus they had met with God himself. Although they would struggle to find words that could adequately express so momentous a claim, the early Christians testified, in the face of widespread ridicule and opposition, that this man from Nazareth was the Lord who made heaven and earth. It is that confession that lies at the heart of Christian faith. In this chapter we will investigate what is involved in making such a claim.

WHO IS JESUS?

Although scholars have debated at great length what precisely we can know about the historical figure of Jesus of Nazareth, there is little doubt that his life and teaching prompted a range of starkly contrasting reactions. Clearly, there was something about him that attracted attention. The gospel writers tell of Jesus attracting great crowds to listen to his teaching; they tell of many who were attracted by his ministry of healing, and of some who weren't used to being shown any favour – the poor, the outcast, the sick and the sinful – who found that they were sought out by Jesus and who encountered in him a compassion that gave them hope in the face of life's hardships and in the face of their own failings. We learn too from the gospel writers that Jesus spoke and acted as though he had 'inside knowledge' about the nature and purposes of God. He spoke regularly of God's coming kingdom and appeared to suggest that he was involved in bringing that kingdom about. That kind of talk infuriated the religious authorities, attracted interest from others and apparently puzzled many. It certainly begged the question 'Who is this man?' That question crops up again and again in the four gospels. It is worth exploring some of the answers that are given.

A CARPENTER'S SON FROM NAZARETH

In the opening chapter of John's gospel we are told of Jesus' early encounters with some of those who would become his disciples. Some reacted positively to Jesus and, as John tells the story, they became convinced almost immediately that Jesus was the Messiah. The Hebrew word for 'Messiah', translated into Greek as 'Christ', means 'God's anointed one'. In Israel's Scriptures, referred to by Christians as the Old Testament, the Messiah was a figure proclaimed by the prophets who would one day come to fulfil God's purposes. These early disciples of Jesus, spoken of in John 1:35–42, were apparently convinced that Jesus was the promised Messiah. But not all were convinced, at least not to begin with. Upon being told that Jesus the son of Joseph was the one of whom Moses and the prophets wrote, Nathanael responded with scepticism: 'Can anything good come out of Nazareth?' (John 1:46).

Behind Nathanael's scepticism lay his knowledge of Nazareth itself, and possibly some knowledge of who Joseph was. Nazareth was an outpost in Galilee, a nondescript little town some considerable distance from the centre of political and religious life in Jerusalem. It seemed to Nathanael to be highly unlikely that God would choose Nazareth as the place from which his anointed one would emerge. Even less likely was it that a carpenter's son should be the anointed one. To Nathanael's mind, this was far too ordinary and unremarkable a beginning for the work of the Messiah. And yet Nathanael's dismissive remark reveals something that is vitally important in Christian faith. Jesus is ordinary! Put more precisely, Jesus is one of us; he is a human being who shares in our weakness, our lowliness, our temptations and our struggles. While there is much else that will also be said of Jesus as the tradition of Christian faith develops, this truth remains essential: Jesus is fully and genuinely human. In the more elevated language of the letter to the Hebrews, the humanity of Jesus is affirmed in this way: 'For we do not have a high priest who is unable to sympathise with our weaknesses, but we have one who in every respect has been tested as we are, yet without sin' (Hebrews 4:15). We will encounter a little later some accounts of who Jesus is that deny or appear to compromise his humanity, but the Christian tradition has judged such denials to be in error. Although Jesus is confessed to be the Lord, he is fully human nevertheless.

A BLASPHEMER?

Early in the gospel of Mark the story is told of four people who hear of Jesus' presence in the town of Capernaum and bring to him a man who was paralysed. Mark's gospel, only a chapter in, has already reported three healings undertaken by Jesus. At this early stage of his ministry, the news that Jesus was able to heal the sick had evidently begun to spread. On encountering the man who was paralysed, and on seeing the faith of his friends, Jesus said to the paralytic, 'Son, your sins are forgiven'. The story continues: 'Now some of the scribes were sitting there, questioning in their hearts, "Why does this fellow speak in this way? It is blasphemy! Who can forgive sins but God alone?"' (Mark 2:6–7). The scribes in Jesus' day were well-educated, literate men who were responsible for the drafting and copying of legal documents and other manuscripts. They also functioned as teachers and advisors in Jewish law. Their allegation of blasphemy was well founded, therefore. These men knew the law! They knew that it was blasphemous to make out that one was God (see John 10:33), or to claim a prerogative that was God's alone, the prerogative, in this case, to forgive sins. Eventually the charge of blasphemy would become a central piece of evidence in the case brought against Jesus in his trial in Jerusalem (see Mark 14:64; Matthew 26:65). But again, the assessment of Jesus delivered by these observers, though dismissive, gives access to a deeper truth. As the story of Jesus' encounter with the paralytic continues, it is revealed, according to Mark's telling of the story, that Jesus does have the authority to forgive: Jesus says, '"But so that you may know that the Son of Man has authority on earth to forgive sins. I say to you, stand up, take your mat and go to your home." And he stood up, and immediately took the mat and went out before all of them' (Mark 2:10–12).

These words and actions of Jesus are provocative. They imply, falsely or not, that Jesus has divine authority, and again they beg the question, who is this man? We have heard the verdict of the scribes: Jesus was a blasphemer. There were others among the observers, however, who reacted differently: 'They were all amazed and glorified God, saying, "We have never seen anything like this"' (Mark 2:12).

ELIJAH, A PROPHET, JOHN THE BAPTIST?

It seems that the question of who Jesus is quickly became the question on everyone's lips. In Mark 8, we read of Jesus journeying with his disciples to the villages of Caesarea Philippi, 'and on the way he asked his disciples, "Who do people say that I am?" And they answered him, "John the Baptist: and others, Elijah; and still others, one of the prophets'" (Mark 8:27–28; see also Matthew 16:13–20).

Surprising though these answers may be, they are nevertheless intelligible within the worldview or framework of thought of the day. Elijah, though long departed from the earth, was thought to be a heavenly figure residing with God. Though strange to our minds, it was apparently plausible, at a popular level at least, to think that Elijah might be sent again by God as a leader for the people. Presumably the same could be true of others of Israel's prophets, and perhaps for John the Baptist. It may be, however, that those who mistook Jesus for John the Baptist had not met either man, had not heard of John the Baptist's death and had simply become confused about who was who among the influential teachers and prophets of the day. Even before the social media of our own time, rumours and misinformation were easily spread.

WHO DO YOU SAY THAT I AM?

Jesus himself, however, makes no comment on what others are saying about him. Instead, he turns the question back upon the disciples themselves: 'But who do you say that I am?' (Mark 8:29). That question, directed explicitly at the disciples, alerts us to an important aspect of any enquiry about the identity of Jesus. The question cannot be one of merely academic interest. The scholarly world has produced numerous writings about how Jesus is understood by Mark or by Luke, or by the apostle Paul and so on. But Jesus' question put to the disciples implies that it is not sufficient merely to fall in with the crowd of public opinion, be it popular or scholarly. The question confronts us personally: 'But who do *you* say that I am?' Jesus invites a personal response. In a book concerned as this one is with 'Christian Theology: The Basics', there can be no question more basic than this: 'Who do *you* say that I am?' There are all sorts of ways of skirting around this question, especially in academic enquiries about Jesus, but in the account of Jesus provided by the New Testament, the personal question is of paramount importance. This point was made again and again by the nineteenth-century Christian thinker Søren Kierkegaard (1813–55). Kierkegaard insisted, in full accord with the New Testament, that Jesus seeks followers, rather than admirers. If it is true, as Christians confess, that Jesus is Lord, then our relation to him cannot be a matter of academic curiosity only. His Lordship calls for discipleship, obedience and, because of the way Jesus exercises his Lordship, it calls also for a response of worship and of love.

The New Testament is, of course, the witness of those who became followers of Jesus, who confessed of him that he is indeed the Messiah, and who left behind their previous lives in order to participate in the reality of the kingdom of God that Jesus both proclaims and sets in train. Returning to the account in Matthew's gospel of the question Jesus puts to his disciples, we are given a glimpse of how that following and how that confession comes about. In response to Jesus' question, Simon Peter, one of the disciples who was with him, said, 'You are the Messiah, the Son of the living God' (Matthew 16:16). This has become, of course, a standard response among followers of Jesus. It is a standard response of those who, after encountering Jesus, feel compelled to confess that God is at work in him, that God is somehow present in him. It is a response of faith, and of commitment. It is important to note, in Matthew's gospel, how Jesus responds to Simon Peter's confession. 'Blessed are you, Simon son of Jonah!' Jesus says. 'For flesh and blood has not revealed this to you but my Father in heaven.' Jesus' response implies that a true understanding of who Jesus is is not the fruit of human investigation. It is not the outcome of some scholarly process in which we determine to undertake our enquiries in the detached and objective manner so often commended by modern scholarship. 'Flesh and blood', says Jesus, 'has not revealed this to you but my Father in heaven.' Understanding of Jesus' identity is portrayed here as the fruit of revelation rather than of human enquiry. God is at work in our knowing of him, giving us eyes to see and minds to understand. The New Testament elaborates this point in various ways. In John's gospel, for instance, Jesus promises that he will send his Spirit, who will bear witness to him and who will guide disciples into all truth (see John 16:12–14, also 14:26). The account given in John's gospel suggests that the truth of Jesus can be understood only as the Spirit of God transforms human thinking and opens people to a way of seeing things that they could not have come to on their own. The apostle Paul in Romans 12:2 speaks about being renewed through the transformation of your minds. This renewal, as discussed in chapter one, is sometimes called conversion; it involves seeing things in a new light, and having one's view of the world transformed under the impact and God's Spirit. The New Testament is the witness of those who have experienced that kind of transformation, and who testify that God has been at work with them, enabling them to see Jesus, and indeed the whole of reality, in a new light.

THE MESSIAH

We have noted already some of the ways in which those who encountered Jesus naturally sought to understand him in terms of where he belonged in the ongoing story of God's dealings with Israel. Some, as we have seen, considered him to be a blasphemer or a false prophet, but those who became followers of Jesus were convinced that Jesus represented the culmination of God's work with Israel, and that this work was now to include Gentiles (non-Jews) as well. It was not immediately obvious how the continuity between Israel and Jesus should be understood. It took some time for the church to work through that issue; we can see in the writings of Paul and in the gospels the attempt being made to express the faith that the same God who had been at work with Israel is now at work in Jesus. It is one of the tragedies of the church's history that the relation between Israel and the Christian community has often deteriorated into animosity and shameful anti-Semitism. As long as the Jewish and the Christian communities remain divided on the question of whether Jesus is truly the promised Messiah of Israel, it is incumbent upon Christians to acknowledge Paul's reproach of any who would forget that Israel remains beloved of God and his insistence that the gifts of God bestowed upon Israel and God's calling of them to be his people remains irrevocable (see Romans 11:28–29).

The use of Old Testament conceptuality to interpret who Jesus is is a process begun, arguably, by Jesus himself. In Mark's gospel, for instance, Jesus himself appeals to the Old Testament tradition to justify the conduct of his disciples (Mark 2:23–28), he accepts the title, 'Son of David' (Mark 10:46–52) and he appears to accept the messianic overtones of the title (Mark 12:35–37). Elsewhere in the gospels, Jesus clearly prefers the title 'Son of Man' among the many titles used of him. This title too is drawn from the Old Testament and is associated with the coming judge. This dependence upon an Old Testament framework of interpretation is apparent in many of the other titles applied to Jesus – Messiah, High Priest, the second Adam, and so on.

Beyond the use of such titles, there are other ways in which the New Testament writers draw upon Old Testament passages to interpret who Jesus is and what he does. Again, this is a process that appears to have begun with Jesus himself. In Luke 4, for instance, we read of Jesus going to the synagogue, reading from the scroll of Isaiah and suggesting that Isaiah's vision of one who is anointed by the Spirit to undertake the work of God applies to his own ministry (Luke 4:16–21). Matthew's gospel too, which is almost certainly written for a Jewish audience, is eager to show the continuity between Jesus and Israel. In his account of Jesus' birth, Matthew draws heavily upon the Exodus tradition of Israel. Jesus is represented as a new Mosaic figure who will lead his people from bondage to freedom. Similarly, the three Old Testament figures of prophet, priest and king feature prominently in the New Testament interpretations of Jesus' person and work.

Not only the words, but also the actions of Jesus are commonly understood in terms of Old Testament conceptuality. Most obviously, Jesus' celebration and reinterpretation of the Passover meal marks a high point in Jesus' self-interpretation and signifies both the new thing that God is doing among his people and its continuity with all that has gone before. Or again, several of the healing miracles that Jesus performs involve a deliberate reference to the established traditions of Israel. 'Go and show yourself to the priest', he says to a leper, 'and offer the gift that Moses commanded' (Matthew 8:1–4). In the story told in John's gospel of the turning of water into wine (John 4), deliberate mention is made of the fact that the water is collected in jars that were set aside for the Jewish rites of purification. That's not an incidental detail but an indication that the transforming work that Jesus does is to be understood in continuity with God's work of purification and transformation already begun in Israel.

These few samples give only a snapshot of the critical importance of the Old Testament in the developing understanding of who Jesus is and what he does, but they indicate a pervasive feature of the New Testament witness, namely that Jesus' person and work are understood in terms of the continuation of the covenant relationship that God had established with Israel, and as the fulfilment of Israel's hope for a coming Messiah.

A DIVERSE WITNESS

It is common to observe that the various New Testament writings exhibit considerable diversity of expression, of emphasis, of historical detail and indeed of theology in their witness to Jesus Christ. Some people take this diversity to be subversive of Christian faith. The claim is made that the New Testament writers' failure to produce a single, definitive account of who Jesus is and what he did undermines the credibility of the New Testament as a whole and of the theological convictions that appear within it and arise from it. Such an attitude requires, however, a glib dismissal of the very considerable unity of purpose that I have referred to above.

The rich diversity of the New Testament texts may be said to strengthen rather than undermine the credibility of their witness. It would be surprising, in fact, if there were not considerable diversity in the New Testament witness. The various writers were seeking for ways against varying backgrounds and in response to particular contextual challenges to find images and titles and modes of speaking through which to communicate the news that Jesus was the promised Messiah and the saviour of the world. In some contexts and for some audiences, an emphasis upon Jesus' continuity with the history of Israel and an expression of the ways in which he was the fulfilment of Israel's hopes would be required. In other contexts, it would be necessary to tell the story of Jesus in ways that could be understood by audiences who spoke Greek and who had relatively little knowledge of Israel's story. Furthermore, as the Christian community grew in numbers and spread throughout the Roman Empire, new objections to the gospel would be encountered and new questions would arise that required fresh explanations and different ways of telling the news of who Jesus is and what he does. The demands of diverse audiences and the differing perspectives of the writers can be seen to shape the way the history of Jesus' life is told by the four gospel writers, and so variations are apparent in historical detail as well. Again, this need not be taken to be subversive of Christian faith. The gospels are renderings of the reality of Jesus. The four gospel writers, like four different artists seeking to portray the same landscape, use different techniques, choose different colours, highlight different aspects of the scene and so on, but that does not preclude them from each providing a trustworthy rendering of the reality of Jesus himself.

JESUS AND HISTORY

Observation of the various ways in which the gospel writers rendered the reality of Jesus gave rise in the nineteenth century to a movement subsequently named the Quest of the historical Jesus. Proponents of this Quest, among whom D. F. Strauss (1808–74) was especially influential, rightly attributed the diversity of the four gospels to the interpretive work of the four gospel writers, but the Questers worried that this interpretive work was liable to distort rather than render faithfully the reality of Jesus himself. They set about the task, therefore, of disentangling the 'historical Jesus' from the so-called 'Christ of faith'. By stripping away the dogmatic or theological interpretation of Jesus by the early church, it was assumed that one could discover Jesus as he really was. The tools employed in this task were the tools of historical enquiry. The detailed story of the progress of this Quest, its demise towards the end of the nineteenth century and its revival in a more sophisticated form in the mid-twentieth century may be read elsewhere. For the moment it is important simply to notice that the Questers assumed that a faithful account of who Jesus was required that theological categories be set aside. The facts of history, it was argued, should be allowed to speak for themselves without being obscured by an overlay of pious devotion to Jesus. The trouble is that the 'facts' of history don't speak for themselves. The data that historians gain access to need to be pieced together and interpreted. Judgements need to be made about what is significant and what is not. It became apparent as the Quest proceeded that those judgements were themselves shaped by the particular beliefs of those who were doing the investigating. The portraits of Jesus that emerged from the Quest reflected to a remarkable degree the prior convictions of those who engaged in the Quest. Strauss's own portrait of Jesus, for instance, was deeply influenced by his commitment to the philosophy of the influential eighteenth-century thinker G. W. F. Hegel (1779–1831). Later Questers developed portraits of Jesus that revealed their own reliance on the thought of the equally influential Immanuel Kant (1724–1804), and so on.

Despite the widely acknowledged failure of the nineteenth-century Quest to present a portrait of Jesus 'as he really was', the Quest did prompt serious theological reflection on whether it really matters whether the gospel writers provide reliable access to the historical figure of Jesus of Nazareth. Some argued, in the wake of the Quest, that it doesn't matter. Rudolf Bultmann, for instance, a German theologian and biblical scholar (1884–1976), was content to regard the gospels as mythological constructions that, despite giving us little information about the Jesus of history, succeed nevertheless in confronting us with the message of God's forgiveness and the challenge of Christian discipleship. One of Bultmann's students, Ernst Käsemann (1906–98), rejected this claim of his teacher and instigated a new Quest for the historical Jesus that sought to demonstrate the continuity between the Jesus of history and the church's confession that this Jesus is the Christ. It mattered to Käsemann, as it has to many other Christian theologians, that the church's confession of Jesus is grounded in the historical reality of Jesus himself. This argument has been developed more recently by another German theologian, Wolfhart Pannenberg (1928–2014), who contends that the methods of historical enquiry must be pressed into the service of Christian faith in order to make clear the continuity between Jesus himself and the theological claims made about him.

While many theologians share this concern that theological confession about Jesus be anchored in historical reality, it is a matter of debate whether historical enquiry, as it is commonly practised, can establish this connection. The difficulty is that historians do not typically employ theological categories in order to account for what they perceive to be going on in history. It might be argued that historians have no competence, as historians, either to utilise or to adjudicate theological claims. Such a line of argument takes us back to Jesus' response to the episode reported in Matthew 16:17: in response to Peter's confession that Jesus is the Messiah, the Son of the Living God, Jesus responds, as discussed above, 'Flesh and blood has not revealed this to you, but my Father in heaven'. Jesus' words appear to indicate that the reality of who he is cannot be properly understood if we limit ourselves to the tools of human enquiry. We have need of the guidance of God. Historical enquiry about Jesus may help us in other ways, but it cannot confirm that Jesus is the Messiah or that he is the Son of the Living God. If that inference from Jesus' response to Peter is true, then the reliability of the gospel's witness to Jesus cannot be established by historical enquiry. The trustworthiness of that witness is a matter of faith, a faith, so Christians might argue, that is itself a gift of God.

A further criticism of the nineteenth-century Quest, made initially by Martin Kähler (1835–1912), is that we cannot in fact disentangle the historical data of Jesus' life from the gospel writers' interpretation of it. The true Jesus, Kähler insisted, is the Christ of Christian proclamation. What is more, we have no access to Jesus except through this proclamation. If this is true, or even largely true, then Christian reflection on the question of who is Jesus ought to proceed by attending in faith to what the New Testament has to say.

MAN WITH US AND GOD AMONGST US

Despite the evident diversity across the four gospels, a striking and decisive point of commonality among them is that the man Jesus of whom they speak has a unique relation to God, in virtue of which the relation of humankind to God, and indeed the relation of the whole creation to God, is restored and renewed. While the various authors are certainly attempting to tell the story of a human being who lived his life for the most part in Galilee and died by crucifixion at the hands of Roman authorities in Jerusalem, they are also convinced that they cannot tell the story of Jesus without utilising theological categories. They are all convinced that to speak the truth about this man they must tell of his relation to God. So, for instance, Mark, the earliest of the four gospels, opens in this way: 'The beginning of the good news of Jesus Christ, the Son of God' (Mark 1:1). Matthew begins with 'An account of the genealogy of Jesus the Messiah, the Son of David, the Son of Abraham' (Matthew 1:1). The genealogy assures the Jewish readers of Matthew's gospel that Jesus is one of them. Luke, incidentally, offers a genealogy that runs back to Adam, thus embracing the whole of the human race. Neither genealogy is a record of strict biological descent. Matthew and Luke intend to assure us, rather, that Jesus is human like us. He is part of humanity's story. Immediately following the genealogy, however, Matthew presents the story of Jesus' conception and birth, the centrepiece of which is the announcement that this child shall be named Emmanuel, which means 'God is with us' (Matthew 1:23). Jesus is a human being, to be sure, but in Matthew's view, he is also related to God in some unique way.

Luke makes the same point. An angel appears to Mary, Jesus' mother, and after announcing that Mary will soon become pregnant, the angel says to her, 'The Holy Spirit will come upon you, and the power of the Most High will overshadow you; therefore the child to be born will be holy; he will be called Son of God' (Luke 1:35). Matthew and Luke both show dependence on the gospel of Mark and perhaps on another source that they both knew, and so there are striking similarities in the way they present the news that the human Jesus is uniquely related to God. John's gospel, however, appears to have been written independently of the other three gospels and so presents the story in a rather different way. John does not have a genealogy tying Jesus into the history of Israel or into the history of humankind. The humanity of Jesus isn't presented in that way but is, we might say, a given. On the other hand, John asserts in a much more emphatic fashion that Jesus comes from God. Echoing the story of creation in Genesis 1, John begins his gospel with these words: 'In the beginning was the Word and the Word was with God, and the Word was God' (John 1:1). John goes on to announce that this Word 'became flesh and lived among us, and we have seen his glory, the glory as of a Father's only son, full of grace and truth' (John 1:14). John then makes clear that this 'Word' who has become flesh is Jesus of Nazareth. He is the full expression of God's glory and grace.

These are, of course, momentous claims. Although the gospel writers did not doubt that Jesus was human, they felt compelled to confess that in encountering Jesus we are confronted with the reality of God. It is John's gospel again that presents this confession in the most emphatic terms. Appearing to the disciples after his resurrection, Jesus shows them the wounds of crucifixion in his hands and in the side of his body. On seeing these wounds in the risen Jesus, Thomas, one of the disciples, confesses, 'My Lord and my God!' (John 20:28). Some scholars have argued that this full ascription of divinity to Jesus is a late development that distorts the earlier belief that Jesus was a prophetic and messianic figure who, though uniquely anointed by God, wasn't actually divine. John was certainly the last of the gospels to be written, sometime in the last decade of the first century, but the 'high Christology' found in John's gospel can also be found in writings that date from a much earlier period. The letter to the Colossians, for instance, probably written in the early 60s, and thus preceding all four gospels, confesses of Jesus that 'He is the image of the invisible God, the firstborn of all creation; for in him all things in heaven and on earth were created, things visible and invisible ... For in him, all the fullness of God was pleased to dwell ... ' (Colossians 1:15–16, 19). Belief in the divinity of Jesus appears to have developed very early in the life of the church. Debates about how belief in Jesus' divinity developed, and whether such belief is consistent with the reality of Jesus himself, have continued through much of the church's history, but the confession that Jesus is both fully human and fully divine lies at the heart of the Christian faith. Put otherwise, the long tradition of Christian faith holds it to be true that 'God was in Christ reconciling the world to himself' (1 Corinthians 5:19). As we shall see in what follows, this confession is undermined if either the humanity or the divinity of Christ is denied.

'High Christology' is a term used to describe conceptions of Jesus that regard him as fully divine, as well as human. 'Low Christologies', on the other hand, emphasise the humanity of Jesus and are less emphatic about Jesus' divinity.

It was inevitable, however, that these claims would be denied. The Christian confession that Jesus, who is one of us, is also the Lord in whom God is uniquely present has continually met with resistance. The standard forms that this resistance has taken emerged very early in Christian history.

CONCEPTUAL DILEMMAS

The most obvious reason for a Greek or a Roman to resist the confession that Jesus is both human and divine was the Hellenistic conception of the world that we have already encountered in chapter two. According to this view, the world is divided into two realms, a temporal and material world that we human beings inhabit, and an eternal, immaterial world that is the realm of the gods. It made no sense to the Hellenistic mind to think of these two worlds intersecting in any way. They were distinct and separate realms. Thus, as we noted in chapter two, the Christian confession that the eternal Word of God had become flesh seemed to be simply absurd. There were people who held fast to this Hellenistic view of things but who were impressed nevertheless by the life and teaching of Jesus and who were willing to share the Christian confession that Jesus was divine. The only way they could do this, however, while also retaining their Hellenistic view of the world was to deny that Jesus was really human.

DOCETISM

The most common attempts to safeguard the divinity of Jesus while denying his humanity are known as Docetism. According to this view the eternal Word of God given to us in Jesus only appeared to be human. His 'humanity' is like a cloak that conceals his true and singular divine nature. It is a mere semblance that enables God to be present in the world but is not essential to the being of Jesus himself. Docetism is a world-denying conceptuality. It devalues the material world in favour of some spiritualised world and contends that the true essence of Christ belongs only to the latter. The historical actuality and particularity of Jesus is incidental to the ideas that he sought to impart. Ancient Docetism has a modern coun-terpart in those who construe the significance of Jesus merely in terms of the ideas he taught. In extreme form, proponents of modern-day Docetism contend that we can adopt the ideas and principles that the biblical Jesus presents to us, even if Jesus himself never actually existed.

The early church, however, opposed such a view. There is in the gospels a remarkable focus on Jesus' participation in the earthy realities of everyday human existence. He is not portrayed merely as the conveyor of high-sounding ideas, but rather as one who is concerned for the poor and the sick and the outcast. He himself enters into their plight. He thirsts and hungers, suffers pain and even death. All of these claims are offensive to the Docetic view, which held that Jesus' eternal soul was unaffected by these bodily travails. Indeed, the true, divine Christ did not die but returned to heaven leaving the shell of

Jesus' body to suffer and die on the cross. Docetism upholds the divinity of Christ but at the expense of his humanity.

EBIONITISM

In contrast with Docetism, the most obvious reason for a Jew to resist the claim that Jesus is both human and divine is Judaism's conviction that there is only one God. While many Jews were willing to accept that Jesus was the Messiah, that he was specially anointed by God to deliver people from the captivity of sin, to confess that he was divine seemed to compromise their belief that there is only one God. That is a genuine problem, for Christians too are monotheists. How can belief in Jesus' divinity, alongside his frequent reference to God, or to his Father – to say nothing yet of the Holy Spirit – be reconciled with the conviction that there is but one God? That is a problem to which we will return in the following chapter. Meanwhile, we need to observe where this monotheistic objection to the divinity of Jesus typically led.

Like Docetism, Ebionitism too is concerned to safeguard the transcendence of God, but it does so in precisely the opposite way, namely by holding to the real humanity of Jesus while denying his divinity. Jesus is confessed to be a prophet who received a unique dignity (not divinity) at his baptism. This bestowal upon him of a unique dignity qualifies Jesus as the Messiah, but his messianic role is confined to the teaching and extension of the law. The Ebionite sect of the first century rejected the writings of the apostle Paul, which seemed to them to accord divine status to Jesus, favoured the gospel of Matthew, which presents Jesus as a successor to Moses, and emphasised the continuing religious and saving significance of the law.

TRULY HUMAN AND TRULY DIVINE

Again, however, this construal of Jesus as truly human but not divine was rejected by the early church. Although it would require the abandonment of the Hellenistic view of the world and a substantial revision of Jewish thinking about God, the early Christians, both Jew and Greek, came to the view that both the humanity and the divinity of Jesus had to be maintained in order to speak truly of who Jesus is.

The 'apostolic tradition' refers to the teaching of the apostles, including the original disciples of Jesus and Paul. This tradition, largely presented in the New Testament, is regarded as authoritative by most branches of the Christian church.

Beyond the writers of the New Testament itself, one of the most important of the early Christian thinkers who sought to defend this view was Irenaeus of Lyon. Again, we have encountered Irenaeus already in chapter two. Irenaeus owed a great deal to the influence of Pauline theology and was a devoted adherent of what he regarded as the apostolic tradition. Irenaeus was concerned, however, at what he perceived to be the largely destructive influence of Greek philosophy on the content of the Christian gospel. He was thus concerned that the gospel should be thought through and articulated in the most rigorous intellectual manner, to hold its own, that is, against the prevailing intellectual culture of the day. Irenaeus considered it of the utmost importance to stress that Jesus Christ was both fully human and fully divine. Unless he was both, Irenaeus insisted, then it made no sense to speak of him as the saviour of humankind. Only if the divine Word entered fully into our human life could the whole of our life be redeemed and reconciled with God. This confession presents us, however, with some formidable conceptual challenges. What implications does it have for the traditional Jewish confession that there is one God who is unchangeable and transcendent? How is it possible to speak of the presence of this same God in the human figure of Jesus of Nazareth who suffered and died on the cross? Does the appearance of God in Christ involve some compromise of God's divinity as traditionally understood?

ARIANISM

These are questions that take us to the heart of the most important debate about Jesus in the early church, a debate sparked off by a priest in Alexandria named Arius (c.250–336). Again influenced by Hellenistic conceptions of the necessary distinction between the divine and the human realms, Arius insisted that the human being Jesus of Nazareth could not be said to possess any of the divine qualities of immortality, sovereignty, perfect wisdom and goodness, immutability and so on. God was understood to possess all these things by definition, and it seemed to Arius to be impossible that a human being could also be said to be eternal, impassible, infinite, omnipotent, omniscient and so on. The only possible conclusion to be drawn was that Jesus was not divine, or, perhaps, not fully divine.

One of the key matters giving rise to the controversy was the claim apparently made by Arius that 'there was a time when the son was not'. The Son is not eternal but was begotten by the Father. While Arius was prepared to accept the confession found in Ephesians 15:18 that Jesus was 'the beginning, the first-born', Jesus belongs nevertheless firmly on the side of creation rather than on the side of God (as imagined in the Greek worldview). Arius did concede, however, that as the firstborn creature, Christ then participated in creating the rest of creation and existed, therefore, 'apart from time before all things'. He received sufficient wisdom and light from God to be able to reveal God, but Jesus did not share in the being of God and did not know him perfectly. Jesus is said to be, in the Arian scheme, a *tertium quid*, a 'third thing' neither fully God, nor fully human, but existing somewhere in between.

What is at stake in the dispute around Arius' theology? The debate concerns whether the reality of God himself is present with us in Jesus. Arius' legitimate concern to safeguard the transcendence of God, to avoid any confusion between the being of the creator and the being of the world, resulted in a theology in which God has no direct contact with his creation but remains remote and isolated from it in the absolute serenity of an unchanging and static perfection. These views of Arius caused considerable controversy in the fourth century. The Roman Emperor Constantine had converted to Christianity in AD 312 and began to take a strong interest in the affairs of the church. Constantine was concerned that the theological dispute would threaten the peace of the Empire, and he called a Council of bishops to resolve the issue. The Council took place in Nicaea in AD 325. It was at this Council that St Athanasius (*c*.296–373), one of the greatest theologians of the early church, came to prominence.

Athanasius argued at the Council that Arius' conception of a remote and utterly transcendent God had very little to do with the God of the Jewish and Christian scriptures. To the question of whether Arius' theology was a faithful interpretation of that biblical witness, Athanasius answered, No! For the Bible speaks of a God who does not remain remote and isolated in the heavenly realm but draws near to his people in covenant love, culminating in the unique presence and activity of Jesus Christ. The impact of the differences between Athanasius and Arius can be seen in relation to two key theological themes, salvation and revelation.

SALVATION

Arius could say, with his opponents, that Christ is our saviour, but salvation in Arius' scheme could not really involve a genuine reconciliation between God and creation. Arius' God remains remote from and uninvolved with the concerns of this world. While Arius considered the world to be redeemed by virtue of the presence within it of the Logos [Jesus], if Jesus is not himself divine, then union with him is not the same thing as reconciliation with God. Whatever salvation might involve in Arius' scheme of things, it has no room for the biblical emphasis upon a genuine reconciliation between God and humanity that enables human beings to live in intimate communion with God (see, e.g., Ephesians 2:13–14).

For Athanasius, the work of salvation involves the comprehensive reconciliation between God and his creation brought about through the incarnation of the divine Word. Reconciliation with God is made possible precisely because God has not remained in glorious isolation but has come to be among us in the person of his Son. Arius' scheme, by comparison, involved the church, Athanasius argued, in nothing short of idolatry. If someone less than God brought about our salvation and was worshipped as the saviour, then we are simply reintroducing a form of pagan polytheism. This was an argument used frequently against Arius. He who wanted to protect the absolute sovereignty and transcendence of God proposed nevertheless to worship a creature alongside God. Arius' theology, Athanasius contended, was thus shown to be incoherent even on its own terms.

REVELATION

A further charge brought against Arius is that his understanding of Jesus Christ as less than fully divine, along with his insistence that Jesus knows the Father only partially and imperfectly, undermines the Christian claim that Jesus reveals the Father. If Arius' view of Jesus is accepted, then God remains largely unknown. The remoteness of God entails a profound gulf between God and humanity that cannot be bridged. Christianity is left with no grounds to say that God is revealed in Christ.

Athanasius was fond of pointing out that for someone who denied that God had appeared among us in Christ, Arius claimed to know a great deal about God. But where had he got this knowledge from? Athanasius himself was in no doubt. Following the lead of the Greek philosophers, Arius had fabricated his concept of God using his own powers of reason. His concept of God was largely predetermined and was little altered by the reality of Jesus. Christian faith holds that we learn through the self-disclosure of God in Christ what can and cannot be said of God. God has made himself known in Christ, and Jesus himself, therefore, must be the criterion of all Christian claims to know and speak of God. Arius, by contrast, finds the criterion for theology in truths determined by Greek cosmology. The theological system is set in stone prior to revelation. The reality of Jesus, therefore, must be made to conform to what we already claim to know about God and about the world. This struck Athanasius as an improper way for Christian theologians to proceed.

It is for these reasons that the church felt compelled to affirm its belief that in the person of Jesus we are encountered by God himself, without compromise of his divinity. Therefore, at the Council held in Nicaea in 325, the gathered bishops and theologians confessed that Jesus is 'God from God, Light from Light, true God from true God, and of one being with the Father'. They sought to emphasise, against the view of Arius and his supporters, that Jesus is fully divine and shares in the same being as the one whom Jesus himself called 'Father'. This was a decisive moment in the development of Christian theology. The formulations of Nicaea were modified slightly at a Council in Constantinople in 381 and are now known as the Nicene Creed. This creed remains, in most branches of the Christian church, an authoritative statement of the church's belief.

There would be more controversy yet in relation to Christ, and it would be necessary to consider much more fully how this belief in the divinity of Christ could be held alongside the monotheism that was also a central tenet of Christian faith. But in the theological formulations of Nicaea, the church had found a way to express the faith, found also in the New Testament, that in Jesus of Nazareth we are encountered by the living God himself. That remains a matter of faith, of course, but such a statement as this lies at the very heart of the Christian understanding of God.

TWO-NATURE CHRISTOLOGY

Several further Councils held over the course of the following two centuries would further debate and refine the church's efforts to proclaim faithfully who Jesus is. While the affirmation of Jesus' divinity had been settled at Constantinople in 381, debate continued about how best to confess together that Jesus, having two natures, was both truly human *and* truly divine. These debates came to a head at a Council held at Chalcedon in 451, at which those present declared, 'we teach ... one and the same Christ, Son, Lord, Only-begotten, known in two natures without confusion, without change, without division, without separation'. In other words, the two natures of Christ, both his humanity and his divinity, were to be affirmed without confusing them, altering them, dividing them or compromising them in any other way.

In arriving at this formulation, the bishops were concerned above all to refute the views of a good number of theologians who were deemed to have got it wrong. These included Apollinarius (c.310–90), who contended that Christ had a human body and a human soul but the human mind was replaced in him by the divine Logos, and Eutyches (c.378–c.454), who declared that Christ had only one nature and that was divine. Apollinarius and Eutyches were Greek-speaking theologians who were influenced by the Hellenistic philosophy we spoke of earlier. They share a tendency of a number of theologians associated with the centre of learning in Alexandria, who emphasised the divinity of Christ at some risk to the humanity. An opposing school of theologians associated with Antioch sought to affirm both the divinity and the humanity of Christ but in ways that risked dividing one from the other. Nestorious, who was Bishop of Constantinople from 428–31, is alleged to have fallen prey to that danger. His account of the two natures of Christ appears to portray Christ as two separate persons united by a merging of wills. This too was deemed to be unsatisfactory, first by a Council held at Ephesus in 431, and then again at Chalcedon. The theological debates and the political manoeuvring of this era in church history were complex and untidy, but these decades of debate spanning the years between the Councils of Nicaea in 325 and Chalcedon in 451 were enormously important for the church as it tried to bring some conceptual clarity to its conviction that in the human person Jesus of Nazareth, God is present, reconciling the world to himself.

In more recent times, the church's conviction that Jesus is both fully human and fully divine has been challenged by some but upheld by others. Among the doubters were a group of theologians who contributed essays on the matter to a book edited by John Hick and published in 1977 under the title *The Myth of God Incarnate*. Some in that book argued that the idea of a divine being coming to earth belongs to a bygone era and must now be regarded as a mythical way of affirming the significance of Jesus, who is nevertheless fully but only human. Others argue that the categories of divinity and humanity are mutually exclusive. If God is eternal, infinite, omniscient (all-knowing), omnipresent (not confined to a particular space) and omnipotent (all-powerful), then it makes no sense to regard a mere human being as divine. There is not space here to examine these arguments in detail. It is important to note, however, that both arguments involve presuppositions that can be challenged. The first argument supposes that belief in the incarnation depends upon a naïve and outmoded view of the world in which human beings inhabit a flat earth while God exists in some heavenly realm up amongst the stars somewhere. It is within the context of that ancient view of the universe that it seemed to make sense to speak of a God coming to earth. So the argument goes. It is first of all doubtful that people of biblical times did subscribe to such an understanding of God's relation to the world, but secondly, people have believed in the incarnation for centuries now while also acknowledging the discoveries of modern science concerning the nature of the universe. This persistence suggests that belief in the incarnation does not in fact depend on the naïve worldview that was supposed to have been held by the biblical writers.

The second argument about the divine attributes of infinitude, omnipresence and so on, being incompatible with the attributes of humanity, has been given careful and extended consideration in the theological tradition. One response to the challenge is known as kenotic

Christology. The term 'kenotic' derives from the Greek word for *kenosis*, meaning emptiness. Drawing especially on Philippians 2:5–8, which speaks of Christ 'emptying himself', it has been argued that Christ sets aside or chooses not to exercise the attributes of divinity. Instead, as Philippians 2 puts it, he humbles himself and takes the form of a slave in order to bring about the divine purpose. It is nevertheless God who acts in this way. Others suggest that this lowliness of Christ, and his adoption of the form of a slave, do not involve any relinquishing of divine capacity but are instead the fullest possible expression of self-giving, omniscient, omnipotent and eternal love.

A further argument commonly advanced by those who deny the unique significance attributed to Jesus on account of his alleged divinity involves recognition of the commendable devotion, theological insight and upright moral living exhibited by people of other faiths. This should dissuade Christians, it is suggested, from attributing unique significance to the Christian way, and to Jesus as saviour. We will return to this matter in chapter six.

SPIRIT CHRISTOLOGY

Appreciation of the traditional claim that Jesus is both human and divine has been strengthened in recent years by attention to the way in which the Spirit is involved in the life of Jesus. The Spirit is said to be present at Jesus' conception, impregnating Mary his mother. The Spirit is present again at Jesus' baptism, descending upon him like a dove and empowering him for the ministry that he is about to undertake (Mark 1:11; Matthew 3:17; Luke 3:22; cf. John 1:32). Not only does Jesus receive the Spirit from God, however, he also gives it to others (Mark 13:11; Matthew 10:20; Luke 12:12; John 20:22). Jesus himself announces the beginning of his ministry with the words 'The Spirit of the Lord is upon me, he has sent me to proclaim release to the captives … ' (Luke 4:18f). Elsewhere Jesus explains the healing miracles he performs by indicating the Spirit's presence; 'Since it is by the Spirit of God that I cast out demons then the kingdom of God has come upon you' (Matthew 12:28). While the Spirit continues to be called the Spirit of God, the Spirit is also frequently designated as the Spirit of the Son (Galatians 4:6), the Spirit of Jesus (Acts 16:7) or the Spirit of Christ (Romans 8:9). The close relationship indicated here between Jesus and the Spirit is characteristic also of the relationships between Jesus and the one he addresses as Father.

As we will explore further in the following chapter, Christians understand the one God in terms of the communion of three persons, Father, Son and Spirit. To speak of the Son's divinity, therefore, is to speak of his intimate communion with the Father and the Spirit. It is this communion that makes him who he is. The claim that Jesus is divine is hard to believe if one imagines Jesus as an isolated human being, but the gospels do not present Jesus in that way. Rather, they make very clear the extent to which Jesus' life is dependent on the Father and upon the Spirit. He does not act alone, but is constantly responsive to the guidance of the Father and the empowerment of the Spirit. So much so, in fact, that it makes sense to say that he is one with them (see, e.g., John 10:30, 17:11).

Yet the New Testament also makes clear that Jesus is one with us. He shares our humanity, knows our weaknesses, experiences our temptations and participates in our struggles, even to the point of suffering and death. By sharing fully in our humanity, the beloved Son of God, empowered by the Spirit, takes our humanity into his communion with the Father. It is by this means that our humanity, broken and distorted by sin, is healed and restored and reconciled with God. A fuller account of this reconciliation will be the subject matter of chapter five.

JESUS CHRIST TODAY

We have spent some time discussing the understanding of Jesus developed in the early church. That is because a range of key issues were thought through in that era that remain important for Christians today. It is vital that Christians be attentive to those who have gone before and who have wrestled with some of the same problems that Christians confront today. It is also important, however, that Christians consider in their own age how to confess the church's faith that in Jesus we are met by the eternal God and are invited to participate in God's work of salvation. New contexts do not demand that a different gospel be proclaimed, but they some-times require new ways of proclaiming the gospel; they sometimes prompt attention to aspects of the biblical witness that had been neglected; and they often serve to correct imbalances or distortions in the church's proclamation of the gospel.

This has surely been the case with the emergence of feminist Christology, which has drawn attention to ways in which the maleness of Jesus has been used to serve patriarchal agendas and to bolster unjust and oppressive social structures. While some feminist theologians have responded by abandoning faith in Christ, others have helped the church to a new understanding of the humanity of Christ that does not privilege his maleness, and to see the extent to which Jesus challenged the patriarchal structures of his own day.

Theologians from Latin America and from Asia, writing very often from situations of suffering and oppression, have helped the church see the 'pain of God' revealed in the suffering Christ. The pain of God is a phrase used especially by the Japanese theologian Kazoh Kitamori (1916–98). Fellow Japanese theologian Kosuke Koyama (1929–2009) likewise emphasises the suffering of Christ and offers a profound reflection on the way of the cross. Koyama contrasts the crucified mind, 'shaken by the foolishness and weakness of God', with the crusading mind of Western Christianity (Koyama, *No Handle on the Cross*, p. 10), and so sheds new light on what following Jesus entails.

The Civil Rights movement in the United States led by Martin Luther King began to speak of Jesus Christ as liberator, as the one who promised freedom to the oppressed. The social and political implications of the Christian gospel were thereby brought into sharp focus. This theme was taken up by King's African American contemporary, James Cone (1938–), who began to speak of a black Christ who could be found amongst the struggle of black Americans for freedom and justice. Likewise, in the context of the struggle against apartheid in South Africa, Christ as liberator became a powerful theme. Allan Aubrey Boesak (1945–) writes, 'Black theology is a theology of liberation ... Black theology believes that liberation is not only "part of" the gospel or "consistent with" the gospel; it is the content and framework of the gospel of Jesus Christ' (Boesak, *Farewell to Innocence*, p. 9).

In many parts of Africa the liberating work of Christ is seen to be relevant not only at the social and political level but also at the personal level. The Ghanaian sociologist and theologian Kofi Appiah-Kubi says that indigenous African churches 'believe that total personal healing of spiritual, psychological and physical man is the gift of God, which he pours on his believing community through Jesus Christ. Christ is seen as being more powerful than any evil power, even though they recognise the existence of such evil powers' (Appiah-Kubi, 'Christology'). Attention to the healing ministry of Jesus and to his victory over evil powers has also been a feature of the Pentecostal and Charismatic movements. Such attention has often been lacking in Western churches, whose participation in a post-Enlightenment culture has made them resistant to the biblical reports of miraculous healing and evil powers.

These examples provide an indication only of how the challenge to respond to Jesus' own question 'Who do you say that I am?' is being taken up in the contemporary world. It is vital that the church continues to respond afresh to that most basic of Christological questions. There is always risk in doing so, the risk that the church's proclamation of Jesus may distort rather than bear faithful witness to who he is. But it is a risk that must be taken if the church is to continue to engage in its calling to proclaim the gospel to the ends of the earth. To guard against distortion, the church must undertake the task of theological reflection; it must return again and again to the witness provided in Scripture and, following the ancient principle that faithful theology begins in prayer, it must let its understanding of Jesus be sustained and nurtured by keeping company with the risen Christ himself.

FOR FURTHER READING

There are numerous books that provide an overview of the various quests for the historical Jesus; see, for example, N. T. Wright, *Who Was Jesus?* (Grand Rapids, MI: Eerdmans, 1993), and Alister E. McGrath, *Christian Theology: An Introduction* (Oxford: Blackwell, 1994), 316–27. In *The Real Jesus* (San Francisco: HarperCollins, 1996), Luke Timothy Johnson provides a scathing critique of the whole enterprise of historical Jesus research.

On the New Testament's presentation of Jesus, see Graham N. Stanton, *The Gospels and Jesus*, 2nd ed. (Oxford: Oxford University Press, 2002), Richard Burridge, *Four Gospels, One Jesus*, 2nd ed. (Grand Rapids, MI: Eerdmans, 2005), or Raymond E. Brown, *An Introduction to New Testament Christology* (New York: Paulist Press, 1994).

Accounts of the early Christological controversies can be found in numerous places. See, for example, Daniel Migliore, *Faith Seeking Understanding* (Grand Rapids, MI: Eerdmans, 1991), Ch. 8., and H. E. W. Turner, *Jesus the Christ* (Oxford: Mowbrays, 1976).

An early article outlining the contours of Spirit Christology is Roger Haight's 'The Case for Spirit Christology', published in *Theological Studies* 53.2 (1992), 257–87.

Although the range of feminist approaches to Christology is broad, a useful introduction to the field can be found in Lisa Isherwood, *Introducing Feminist Christologies* (London: Sheffield Academic Press, 2001), while a couple of contrasting feminist approaches can be seen in Rosemary Radford Ruether's *To Change the World: Christology and Cultural Criticism* (London: SCM Press, 1981) and Patricia Wilson Kastner's *Faith, Feminism and the Christ* (Philadelphia: Fortress Press, 1983).

Approaches to Christology from an Asian context may be found in Kosuke Koyama, *No Handle on the Cross: An Asian Meditation on the Crucified Mind* (London: SCM Press, 1976), and in Chung Hyun Kyung's essay 'Who Is Jesus for Asian Women?' in her book *Struggle to be the Sun Again: Introducing Asian Women's Theology* (London: SCM Press, 1991), 53–73.

Approaches from African perspectives to the question 'Who is Jesus?' are outlined in Mercy Amba Oduyoye, 'Jesus Christ', in *The Cambridge Companion to Feminist Theology*, edited by Susan Frank Parsons (Cambridge: Cambridge University Press, 2002), 151–70.

THE TRIUNE GOD

The foundational conviction of Christian faith is that God is present with humanity in and through the person of Jesus of Nazareth. In Jesus Christ, God gives himself to be known in person, is present with humanity, and participates in human history in order to restore and heal the relationship between God and all that he has made. Everything that Christian theology has to say about God arises from this confession and from the reality to which it points.

In the preceding chapter we surveyed the New Testament witness to Jesus, in the light of which it makes sense to say that Jesus is one with the Father and with the Spirit. The identity of this human being, we noted, is inseparably bound up with his relation to God. Recognising this, the disciple Thomas, on seeing the risen Christ, addresses him as 'My Lord and my God'. This ascription of divinity to Jesus, and elsewhere to the Spirit, is central to Christian faith and yet gives rise to a rather important theological problem. The Christian church claims to be monotheistic. That is to say, Christians believe in one God. They wish to remain faithful to this fundamental conviction that is inherited from Judaism. How is it possible to remain monotheistic, however, when the divinity of three persons, the Father, the Son and the Holy Spirit, is being asserted? What is involved in confessing, as Christians do, that they believe in one God, Father, Son and Holy Spirit?

BIBLICAL ROOTS OF THE DOCTRINE
OF THE TRINITY

Let us begin again with the biblical background. It is true to say that there is no doctrine of the Trinity as such in the Scriptures of either the Jewish or the Christian faiths. Christian theology contends, however, not that the doctrine can be simply read off the pages of Scripture, but rather that the Trinitarian understanding of God arises from a faithful interpretation of the biblical story. Let us see how that works out.

THE HEBREW SCRIPTURES

One of the most fundamental theological convictions of the Jewish people is that God engages with Israel in person and that the character of that engagement is determined by God's steadfast love. God is known to Israel as the one who establishes a covenant with them, who delivers them from bondage in the land of Egypt, who promised them a land in which to dwell and who gave them a law. God is the one who speaks to Israel through its prophets and who meets them in their worship. Throughout all of this, God's existence is never a matter of dispute. What is in question instead is the extent to which God and Israel respectively are faithful to the covenant relationship that binds them together. Again and again, while God remains faithful, Israel falls short of God's calling to live as his covenant people. Thus, we find a tradition of judgement upon Israel in which Israel is called to account for its unfaithfulness.

> The word of the Lord came to me:
> You, O mortal, thus says the Lord God to the land of Israel:
> An end! The end has come upon the four corners of the land.
> Now the end is upon you,
> I will let loose my anger upon you;
> I will judge you according to your ways.
> I will punish you for all your abominations.
>
> (Ezekiel 7:1–3)

These words from Ezekiel are but one example. Again and again, however, God's judgement and his wrath are tempered by his mercy. Again and again, the covenant is maintained, Israel is restored and the people are given a chance to begin anew.

It is not just Israel's side of the covenant that is called into question, however. In the Psalms, for instance, Israel pleads with God and calls God to account.

> O God, you have rejected us, broken our defences;
> you have been angry; now restore us!
> You have caused the land to quake; you have torn it open;
> repair the cracks in it for it is tottering.
> You have made your people suffer hard things;
> you have given us wine to drink that made us reel.
>
> (Psalm 60:1–3)

This tradition of lament before God continued in the twentieth century, perhaps with greatest cause in that century. Elie Wiesel, for instance, a Jewish author who spent his boyhood in the concentration camps of Nazi Germany, writes:

> There were many periods in our past when we had every right in the world to turn to God and say, "Enough. Since You seem to approve of all these persecutions, all these outrages, have it Your way; let Your world go on without Jews. Either You are our partner in history, or You are not. If You are, do Your share; if You are not, we consider ourselves free of past commitments. Since You choose to break the Covenant, so be it."
>
> And yet, and yet … We went on believing, hoping, invoking His name … We did not give up on Him.
>
> (Wiesel, A Jew Today, p. 164)

It is important to notice what is involved theologically in such material as this. There is an absolute conviction that God is involved with his people and is involved with history. This is a view that contrasts sharply with the ideas of God in classical Greek philosophy. As we have seen earlier, according to the Greek philosophers God was a remote principle of order in the universe, uninvolved with the temporal world of change and history and seeking no engagement with humanity itself.

There are at least three offences to the Greek mind in the Hebrew tradition of lamentation such as we have seen in the book of Psalms and more recently in the writings of Elie Wiesel. The first is the notion that God is personal and is the dialogue partner of humanity. The second is the suggestion that God's way with humanity may be called into question, and the third is the conviction that history may be the terrain of God's self-disclosure.

Why is this important? It is important because it is within the Hebrew tradition of thought and not within the tradition of Greek philosophy that it is intellectually conceivable to speak of God's being present within us in person. The Trinitarian understanding of God is based on the conviction that God is known in person, that God participates in history and communicates with his people. Through his Spirit and his Word, God makes himself known and draws people into relationship with himself. Although the Jewish Scriptures do not themselves have any such thing as a doctrine of the Trinity, it was nevertheless in Hebrew soil that such an understanding of God was able to grow.

THE NEW TESTAMENT

Moving on to the New Testament, then, and to the story told there of the God who has come among us in human flesh, there is no surprise to the Hebrew mind that God should send a saviour to deliver his people from bondage, but those Jews who were drawn to Jesus as the Messiah and who became his disciples felt compelled to go beyond the expectation that God would appoint someone to act on his behalf. They confessed instead that God himself had come among them in Jesus. If this were true, then it demanded a revolution in their understanding of God. Although the new understanding would not be expressed with any great conceptual precision until the fourth century – and even then, it is clear that theological formulations are hardly able to do justice to God's self-disclosure in Jesus Christ – the impact of this new theology is already to be seen in the New Testament itself.

When the New Testament speaks of God, and when Jesus himself spoke of 'his Father', there is no question that the one referred to is the same one who is understood to have brought the world into being and who has acted throughout the history of Israel. By and large the insights of Hebrew theology are retained; God exists in covenant relationship with his people; he is loving and forgiving towards them; he speaks through the prophets, and guides through history; he judges and he has mercy and he promises the fulfilment of his purposes in the kingdom of God. What is new in the New Testament is that all these things are qualified and brought to a particular focus and fulfilment in Jesus Christ and in such a way as to elicit from those who were his disciples the confession that in encountering Jesus they were entering into communion with the Holy God himself. This Jesus who had come among them spoke and acted with the authority of God himself, and he claimed for himself prerogatives that were thought to have belonged to God alone. He forgave sins, placed himself above the law of Moses and declared the coming of God's kingdom in and through his own action.

At the same time, however, Jesus spoke to and of his 'Father' and promised to send the Spirit, each of whom were distinct from Jesus himself and yet were apparently intimately related to him. Whether Jesus said it himself or whether it forms part of the interpretative activity of the early church, it seemed appropriate for Jesus to say, 'the Father and I are one' and 'whoever has seen me has seen the Father'. Further indication of a unique unity between God the Father and Jesus, a unity that also includes the Spirit, is given through Jesus' promise: 'I will send you from the Father – the Spirit of truth that issues from the Father – he will bear witness to me' (John 15:26).

A new theology is emerging in these New Testament texts, a theology that regards the Word and Spirit referred to in the Old Testament not merely as energies emanating from God, but rather as distinct persons in a threefold expression of God's being. This threefold expression does not indicate, however, merely a differentiation between three ways in which God acts. It is not as though God sometimes acts in a fatherly way, sometimes in a Spirit-like way and sometimes in a Christ-like way. That misunderstanding, called 'modalism' or Sabellianism, after Sabellius, a third-century priest who allegedly taught a form of modalism, came to be regarded as heretical. By contrast, the threefold form of God's self-disclosure is best understood in terms of the action of three persons. That Jesus speaks of the Father and Spirit as though they are distinct from him, while also indicating that they are intimately related to one another and act always in concert, provides the justification for this differentiation. We are dealing here, not with three different 'faces' of a single person, but with three persons intimately related to one another in a way that safeguards the conviction of Old Testament theology that there is only one true God.

The New Testament portrayal of the Father, the Son and the Spirit indicates clearly that they are not isolated individuals doing their own thing, but that they belong together. Their actions *together* are to be seen as the one action of God. While we may speak, therefore, of a differentiation between Father, Son and Spirit, Christian theologians have considered it to be equally important, on the basis of Jesus' own life and teaching, to speak of a fundamental unity between the three persons. There is unity in diversity here, a unity that is something much more profound than the reaching of a common mind or an agreement between persons. The unity between Father, Son and Spirit seems to reside at the level of their very being. That is the impression given by the New Testament, but there remains the challenge of trying to give some intellectual clarity to this notion of a God who is at once both three and one.

CLASSICAL TRINITARIAN THEOLOGY

IRENAEUS OF LYON

The initial response to this theological challenge came again from Irenaeus of Lyon, a theologian whom we have encountered already through his opposition to Hellenistic ways of misconstruing the biblical witness. Irenaeus was the first Christian theologian to follow through to an explicit Trinitarian theology the implications of the biblical witness to God's action in Jesus Christ and the Spirit. Irenaeus contended that the Son and the Spirit may be seen as the two hands of God active in creation and redemption. He equates the Son and Spirit, respectively, with the Word and Spirit of the Old Testament and refers to them both as the 'offspring and similitude' of God. There is, admittedly, a much stronger emphasis upon the unity of God in Irenaeus' metaphor of the two hands than there is upon the distinction of the persons, but Irenaeus does succeed in safeguarding the biblical conviction that wherever the Word and the Spirit are at work in the world, there God himself is present. Whatever inadequacies there may be in Irenaeus' metaphor, his is the first systematic attempt to work out what is involved for our understanding of God in the idea that God the Father is made known to us in Jesus Christ and through the Holy Spirit. His is the first attempt to say that while God is disclosed to us through these three persons, it is nevertheless the one God who acts in and through each of them.

TERTULLIAN

A further step in the development of Trinitarian theology was taken by the North African theologian Tertullian, who was the first to coin the term 'Trinity' or 'Trinitas' as a means of speaking about God. Like Irenaeus, Tertullian also sought to hold together both the threeness and the oneness of God, and he attempted to do so by speaking of three persons and one substance. The term 'substance' used here (*substantia* in Latin) does not refer to something physical or material but rather to the essence, or the essential being, of God. As was often the case in the theological developments of the early church, Tertullian's theology was developed in opposition to two misunderstandings, so he thought, of the biblical witness. He writes against Praxeas who, a little earlier than Sabellius, apparently rejected the view that the Father, the Son and the Spirit are distinct persons. Tertullian insisted that Praxeas' view was a false interpretation of what was going on in the biblical account of God's nature and being. Father, Son and Spirit, Tertullian argued, should be properly distinguished. Contending against the opposite error of separating the persons of the Trinity, Tertullian opposed the Gnostics, particularly Valentinus, who regarded the Son and the Spirit as lesser divinities emanating from the divine. Tertullian again insisted that this was a corruption of the New Testament witness that speaks of the unity of Father, Son and Spirit. As Tertullian himself put it: 'I testify that the Father, and the Son, and the Spirit are inseparable from each other ... [and yet] They are distinct from Each Other' (Tertullian, *Against Praxeas*, ch. 9).

THE COUNCIL OF NICAEA

The next major step forward came with the Council of Nicaea in 325 which, as noted in chapter three, was called in response to a dispute about the person of Christ. On one side of the dispute, Arius, heavily influenced by his Greek conceptuality, insisted that

God could not be identified with the person of Christ. It was an intellectual offence to Arius' Greek mind that God should be considered to be involved in human history. To speak of God in such a way was a contradiction in terms, violating the Greek idea of a remote, eternal, unchangeable and utterly transcendent God. Against Arius, however, the church at Nicaea confessed its faith that Jesus was the true God from the true God and of one being with the Father. In Jesus Christ, God himself has come among us. His Word has taken human form without ceasing to be fully divine. These affirmations about the person of Jesus Christ involve the basic Trinitarian conviction that while it was necessary to speak of the divinity of Christ and also of the divinity of the one whom Christ himself called Father, it was also the case that the life of these two persons, along with that of the Holy Spirit, are so closely bound up together that we must speak of them as one. Although the bishops and theologians who gathered at Nicaea had very little to say about the Holy Spirit, the later Council at Constantinople in 381 made explicit the implication that the Spirit too must be regarded as 'of one being' with the Father and the Son.

ATHANASIUS

One of the champions of this Nicaean theology was the theologian Athanasius. While Athanasius was concerned particularly to defend the idea of the divinity of Christ against a determined Arian opposition, this involved him also in further reflection upon the doctrine of the Trinity. I have been speaking throughout this chapter of three *persons* in God, Father, Son and Spirit, but it was not really until the time of Athanasius that the language of personhood became an acceptable way of speaking of the Trinity throughout the early church. Tertullian, in the early third century, as we have seen, had spoken in Latin of three *personae* in one *substantia*, but the Greek-speaking theologians of the East did not adopt similar language until the late fourth century. At a Synod held in Alexandria, under the leadership of Athanasius, it was agreed that to speak of God as 'three persons in one being' was an appropriate way to express both the threeness and the oneness of God. The Synod was influenced in this decision by the efforts of three theologians from Cappadocia, collectively known as the Cappadocian fathers.

THE CAPPADOCIAN FATHERS

Gregory of Nyssa (*c*.335–*c*.395)
Gregory Nazianzus (*c*.330–*c*.389)
Basil of Caesarea (*c*.330–379)

Echoing in Greek Tertullian's much earlier Latin expression, these three theologians spoke of three persons (*hypostases*) and one being or substance (*ousia*). Acceptance of this terminology in the Eastern church marked a breakthrough in the debate and a degree of consensus between the Latin-speaking Western church and the Greek-speaking Eastern church. The newly accepted terminology allowed for a coherent explanation of the Triune God that safeguarded the unity of Father, Son and Spirit while also expressing the distinction between the three persons.

> During the early centuries of the church's life, a number of theological distinctions emerged between the Greek-speaking churches to the east and Latin-speaking churches to the west. The growing distinctiveness of the two regions in their approaches to questions of church authority eventually led in the eleventh century to the split between the Eastern Orthodox church centred around Constantinople (now Istanbul) and the Western church centred around Rome.

In addition to their talk of God being three persons in one being, the Cappadocian theologians, in particular Gregory Nazianzus, introduced another Greek term that gives expression to the dynamism of the Triune life. The term *perichoresis*, a combination of *peri*, meaning 'around', and *chorein*, which can mean 'to make room for', describes the mutual indwelling or coinherence of each person in the others. It testifies to the intimate fellowship shared by the persons of the Trinity and their mutual dependence upon one another. More simply put, the life of the Triune God is a communion of mutual love in which the distinct identity of each of the three persons is determined by their relationship to the other two. The idea of *perichoresis* prevents distinction or differentiation between the persons from dissolving into separation or division.

AUGUSTINE

One further figure from this period deserves mention. He is Augustine of Hippo (354–430), another Latin-speaking theologian from North Africa. Although he did not use the Greek term *perichoresis*, Augustine's discussion of the Trinity captures something of the same sense. He speaks of the Trinity as a 'society of love' and so emphasises the intimacy and the dynamic and relational nature of God's being. In his efforts to explain the logic of the Trinity, in which three distinct entities nevertheless exist in inseparable unity, Augustine looked to human beings made in God's image and found what he took to be an image of the Trinity in the human mind, in which there is memory, understanding and will. This 'vestige' of the Trinity, as Augustine calls it, gives us an inkling of the threefold differentiation of the one God. Many have doubted the usefulness of Augustine's attempt to find analogies in creation of the Triune being of God. Some analogies have been suggested that are quite misleading, such as, for example, the suggestion that the threeness of God is analogous to the three forms in which water can exist as solid ice, liquid water, and vapour. This is simply modalism, a view that the church long ago rejected. More promising perhaps is the reality of a musical triad, a chord made up of three notes that remain distinct and yet, through their sounding together, they constitute a unity whose rich harmony is a function of their interdependence. Whatever the value of such analogies, the Triune nature of God is best understood by attending to the relation between Father, Son and Spirit, as it is narrated in the New Testament.

Although a great deal of theological jargon has been used in the church's efforts to speak faithfully of the Triune God, the fundamental concern of Trinitarian theology is always to safeguard the experience of Christians that God does not live in glorious isolation as some remote and static being but draws near to humanity in love. The doctrine of the Trinity is a means of expressing the faith that God is present with us through his Word and his Spirit as the true outworking of his own being as love.

THE IMMANENT AND THE ECONOMIC TRINITY

It is necessary here to introduce a further piece of theological jargon. To speak of God's presence with us is to speak of the divine

economy. It is to speak of the ways in which God creates and
sustains and redeems humanity, along with the whole of creation.
The *economic* being of God refers to the ways that God is at work in
the world, to the ways in which God makes himself present to us
and communicates with us. The economic being of God is thus
distinguished from the *immanent* being of God, from the way God
is in himself, independent of the world. Why is it necessary to speak
of God in these two ways? It is necessary because God is free. That
is to say, although God has committed himself to the world in
unconditional love, his being is not in any way dependent on the
world. He is in himself entirely self-contained and self-sufficient.
Talk of the immanent being of God safeguards this point. Despite
his intrinsic self-sufficiency, however, God determines that there
should be something other than himself. He creates a world, and
so God is not only in and for himself but for us, for the creature
whom he loves. He creates space for us, establishes a covenant with
us, sustains our life through the gift of his Spirit, reveals himself
to us and, in response to our waywardness, God reconciles us to
himself. All of this action by God is called the divine economy, and
it is precisely through that economy that we encounter God in his
true nature. We encounter God as he really is in himself. In order
to avoid any suggestion that God's being is somehow dependent on
the world, it is important to distinguish carefully between God's
being in himself and his being for us, but, as it turns out, the God
made known to us in the economy, through Christ and through
the Spirit, is exactly the same God who is above and beyond and
precedes all things. There is no hidden or different God lurking
behind the God who has come among us in Christ and who draws
us into his presence through the working of the Holy Spirit. While
it is true that our human minds cannot comprehend the fullness
of the eternal and infinite God – for now, we know only in part
(1 Corinthians 13:12) – the doctrine of the Trinity affirms that God
is truly revealed in Christ.

FALSE TURNS IN TRINITARIAN THEOLOGY

The doctrine of the Trinity is, admittedly, a difficult concept to
grasp. Sometimes in the church's history there have been theologians whose articulation of the doctrine has been judged to be

inadequate in one way or another. We have already met modalism, the view that the three 'persons' are really just three masks or three ways in which the one God appears to us. Modalism fails to understand the genuine, personal distinction between Father, Son and Spirit. It is likewise possible to misunderstand the genuine unity of the three persons. This failure is known as Tritheism. This is the idea that Father, Son and Spirit are three distinct gods rather than three persons in one being. This destroys the monotheism that is central to Christian theology. It is very unusual to find a Christian theologian who openly advocates tritheism. More commonly the allegation of tritheism is levelled against theologians who set out to give an orthodox account of the Trinity but whose formulations do not safeguard sufficiently well the oneness of God's being. John Philoponus (c.490–c.570), who in other respects contributed much to the Christian theological tradition, is one whose writings on the Trinity erred in this direction. The allegation of tritheism has been, however, a major criticism levelled against Christianity by the religion of Islam. While Christian theologians repeatedly deny it, Muslims tend to see the doctrine of the Trinity as a compromise of the strict monotheism professed by all three of the Abrahamic faiths, namely Judaism, Christianity and Islam.

The Abrahamic faiths are so called because although the three of them, Judaism, Christianity and Islam, have taken different paths, they all trace their origins to God's call to Abraham and Sarah to set out from their land of origin and to be formed into a new people.

A third problem, briefly referred to above, is subordinationism. This is the idea that there is some sort of hierarchy in God. The Father is truly God, while the Son and the Spirit are something a little lower, or subordinate. This is a view found in the Gnostic idea of the Son and Spirit as emanations from the one perfect divine being, and again in Arius, who conceived of the Son's divinity as something less than that of the Father. Subordinationism, in this ontological sense (in a sense that regards the Son and Spirit as lesser beings), contradicts the orthodox conviction that Father, Son and Spirit are equal in their shared divinity and exist together in the mutual and non-hierarchical relation of perfect love.

MODERN TRINITARIAN THEOLOGY

Since the conceptual clarifications worked out in the fourth century, it has been taken for granted in Christian understanding that God is Father, Son and Spirit. The liturgies of the church through the Roman Catholic, Orthodox and Protestant traditions have all preserved this Trinitarian understanding of God's being and yet, in the tradition of Christian theology, the doctrine of the Trinity has often been neglected. That is to say, the Triune understanding of God has had little material effect on how the tradition has expressed or understood other doctrines of the faith, the doctrine of creation for example, or the doctrine of the church. This has not been universally true of the tradition, but it has been a common failing. A number of recent works, including Michael Buckley's *At the Origins of Modern Atheism* and Colin Gunton's *The Triune Creator*, reveal the adverse effects that this neglect has had on Christian theology and its engagement with the world. It has reduced the doctrine of the Trinity to a puzzling appendage to Christian faith that doesn't seem to have much relevance to the everyday life of the Christian. Yet if the Trinity is neglected, it becomes impossible to give a coherent account of the way in which the God who created all things and will bring them to completion at the last has come among us in Jesus, overcomes sin and death, gathers us into communion with him through the Spirit and equips the church to share in the proclamation and in the coming of God's kingdom. Put simply, everything about God's involvement with the world and his equipping of the church to be his people requires a Trinitarian explanation if it is to be properly understood. In our own time two theologians in particular have helped recover an awareness of the indispensability of Trinitarian theology for a proper articulation of Christian faith.

KARL BARTH (1886–1968)

Disillusioned with the theological work of his teachers, who had tended to relegate God to a remote singular being who is known to humanity not in person, but as the distant guarantor of moral order in the universe, Karl Barth returned to the Bible and found there the story of the God who, as we emphasised earlier, draws near to his people in love, enters into their history, suffers with them and gives himself for them in order to bring about their salvation.

This is where we must begin, Barth insisted; we start out from the fact that through His Word God has actually made himself known … (see Barth, *Church Dogmatics*, II.ii, p. 4). But this event of revelation has a threefold structure. God is the one who sends (the Father), he is the one who is sent (the Son) and he is the one who draws us into fellowship with this Word and enables our apprehension of it (the Spirit). God is thus the Revealer, the Revealed and the Revealedness. While the term 'Revealedness' is somewhat clumsy, Barth uses it to emphasise God's involvement in our apprehension of himself. God the Father sends the Son, his own Word in person, and by the power of the Spirit he brings humanity to know him and to enter into loving communion with him. This is the reality with which we are confronted in Jesus, and the starting point, Barth insists, for all that Christian theology has to say about God. The doctrine of the Trinity, for Barth, and the narrative of the Triune God's self-disclosure is not an appendage to be found at some distance from the central subject matter of Christian theology. The self-disclosure of God through Word and Spirit is itself the central subject matter of theology.

KARL RAHNER (1904–84)

The pioneer among Roman Catholic theologians of this new interest in the doctrine of the Trinity was Karl Rahner. Retracing the same steps as the early theologians of the church, Rahner argued that the foundation of Trinitarian faith is to be found in the history of God's salvific dealings with humankind. The basic theological question Rahner is concerned with is whether God remains remote and silent or whether he draws near and speaks. That question, Rahner argues, is decisively answered in Jesus Christ, the one in whom God comes to us in person. Rahner frequently points out that God does not want to offer us anything other than himself in revelation. The event of revelation is the gift of God's own being, and in that event God is the Giver, the Gift and the Giveness. These three terms correspond to the Father, the Son and the Spirit and echo Barth's identification of God as the Revealer, the Revealed and the Revealedness. Rahner sums up the importance of the Trinity as follows:

> It is only through this doctrine that we can take with radical seriousness and maintain without qualifications the simple statement which is at once so very incomprehensible and so very self-evident, namely that God himself as the abiding and Holy Mystery, as the incomprehensible ground of man's transcendent existence is not only the God of infinite distance, but also wants to be the God of absolute closeness in a true self-communication, and he is present in this way in the spiritual depths of our existence as well as in the concreteness of our corporeal history. Here lies the real meaning of the doctrine of the Trinity.
>
> (Rahner, *Foundations of Christian Faith*, p. 137)

With this return to Trinitarian thinking in twentieth-century theology, we are in the process of recapitulating the fundamental insights of the biblical writers who saw clearly that in Jesus of Nazareth, God has come among us, has given himself to be known and redemptively draws the world into communion with himself. The structure of this event is Trinitarian; God the Father gives himself to be known in Jesus Christ the Son through the power of the Holy Spirit. In and through this event, humanity is enabled to know, to speak of and to live in communion with God. In her influential work *God for Us: The Trinity and Christian Life*, Catherine Mowry LaCugna insists that the doctrine of the Trinity cannot be properly understood except in its connection to the saving work of God. Although some critics have worried that LaCugna's exposition of this point sacrifices the distinctness of the immanent being of God, the point is an important one nevertheless. Increasing numbers of contemporary theologians have come to the view that we cannot tell this story of God's involvement in creation and in redemption without speaking of God in Trinitarian terms, and we cannot know truly who God is without attending to the work of God in creation and redemption.

FEMINIST CONCERNS ABOUT TRINITARIAN LANGUAGE

Throughout this chapter I have used the names 'Father, Son and Spirit' to speak of the Triune God. This is, after all, the language we find in the New Testament. For many people today, however, and especially for many women, that language is an obstacle. It suggests that God is male and underwrites patriarchal social arrangements in which the male is dominant and women are thought to be inferior. The feminist theologian Mary Daly put the problem succinctly: 'If God is male then the male is God' (Daly, *Beyond God the Father*, p. 19). As a matter of logic that proposition doesn't work very well, but as an indication of the way males have tended to assume their superiority over women, the proposition makes a telling point. Daly's allegation that human history is saturated with patriarchal assumptions and practices is aimed with some justification at Christianity. There is no denying that the Christian tradition has been guilty of oppressing women and of asserting the superiority of men. It is also true that the maleness of Jesus in particular, along with the maleness of his disciples, has been offered as a theological justification for such oppression. When it is suggested, therefore, that the naming of God as Father, Son (and Spirit) has undergirded patriarchal attitudes and social structures, there is undoubtedly a case to be answered.

This book began with an admission that there is an awkwardness about the male language that Christianity uses to speak of God. Such language has clearly been deeply off-putting for some. In Alice Walker's novel *The Color Purple*, one of the characters, Shug, a black woman, declares, 'When I found out I thought God was white and a man, I lost interest' (Walker, *The Color Purple*, p. 177). However much it may be asserted, quite correctly, that God is not white and God is not male, with respect to the maleness at least, the traditional language of Trinitarian theology is bound to suggest otherwise. The challenge posed by feminism to the patriarchal structures of society and to the patriarchal elements within Christian tradition must be acknowledged, and continuing effort is required to dismantle these structures of oppression and to ensure that all people, male and female, Jew and Greek, black and white, to name just a few categories of human distinctiveness, are enabled to flourish under the conditions of freedom and reconciliation promised in Christ. While there is not space here to respond adequately to the full scope of the feminist critique, two comments about the language used of the divine persons are in order. First, it is important that attempts be made to use a broader range of biblical language in order to speak of God. The Bible does occasionally speak of God using feminine imagery, and there are a wealth of terms used of God that do not carry gendered overtones. It is wholly legitimate, for example, to speak of God as Creator, Redeemer and Sustainer, and we should be prepared to do so. But these terms and others like them don't substitute exactly for the terms Father, Son and Spirit. To begin with, the work of creation and of redemption, and the work of sustaining life, is not exclusively the work of the Father or of the Son or of the Spirit. Each of these works are undertaken by Father, Son and Spirit together, so that the terms Creator, Redeemer and Sustainer do not correspond precisely to the names Father, Son and Spirit. Nor do they do as well at pointing to the personal relations of the Godhead. They indicate functions better than they indicate persons. That's not wrong, but it is not enough. The personhood of Father, Son and Spirit is crucial to a Christian understanding of God. The feminist theologian Valerie Karras, writing from an Eastern Orthodox perspective, likewise argues that the traditional naming of God as Father, Son and Spirit recognises more effectively than the alternatives the personal nature of God (see Karras, 'Eschatology', p. 248).

The second comment, offered in response to the feminist critique, concerns the way that theological language refers to the reality to which it bears witness. One might suppose that in calling God Father, we are implying that God is like a human father. That would entail in turn that human fathers are somewhat like God. In order to understand what God is like, therefore, we should look to the way human fathers behave. Theologically, that is disastrous. Human fathers can be loving and tender and forgiving – they often are, but they can also be impatient, abusive and brutal. How are we to decide which of these attributes reveal the nature of God? The inadequacy of this analogous approach seems to lie behind Jesus' instruction to the crowds and to the disciples that they should 'call no one your father on earth, for you have one Father – the one in heaven'. He goes on to insist that 'the greatest among you will be your servant' (Matthew 23:9, 11). We see here and in the broader passage in Matthew 23 both a radical overturning of the patriarchal relations that are typically found in human society, and Jesus' insistence that the Fatherhood of God is without comparison in the human realm. To discover what the Fatherhood of God looks like, we need to attend to the relationship that Jesus has with the one he calls Father. It turns out that patriarchal domination and oppression have no basis in the way that Fatherhood is exercised by God. The same theological disruption of the common meaning of words takes place in relation to the term Lord, for example. Whoever heard of a Lord who set aside power, who takes the form of a slave and who washes his disciples' feet? But that is what Lordship looks like when it is exercised by Jesus Christ. There can be no more telling critique of the ways in which males have tended to lord it over women and to assert their own superiority. Recognition of the true and unique Fatherhood and the true Lordship of God – two terms that have particularly troubled feminist theologians – may in fact be a means of exposing the falsity and indeed the sinfulness of all male pretensions to patriarchy and domination.

The two comments offered here will not allay entirely the legitimate concern of feminist theologians that the traditional, Trinitarian language of God is prone to deeply problematic interpretations, but it may serve to remind us that a true understanding of who God is and what God is really like can be gained only by attending again and again to God's self-disclosure in the events that the gospels narrate.

FOR FURTHER READING

Useful general accounts of the doctrine of the Trinity can be found in Daniel Migliore, *Faith Seeking Understanding* (Grand Rapids, MI: Eerdmans, 1991), ch. 4; in Patricia Wilson Kastner, *Faith, Feminism and the Christ* (Philadelphia: Fortress Press, 1983), ch. 6; and in Fred Sanders, 'The Trinity', in *Mapping Modern Theology: A Thematic and Historical Introduction*, edited by Kelly M. Kapic and Bruce L. McCormack (Grand Rapids, MI: Baker Academic, 2012), 21–45. More specific accounts of how the doctrine of the Trinity is crucial for the understanding of other areas of Christian doctrine are provided in Jürgen Moltmann's book *The Trinity and the Kingdom: The Doctrine of God* (London: SCM Press, 1981) and in two works by Colin Gunton, *The Promise of Trinitarian Theology*, 2nd ed. (Edinburgh: T&T Clark, 1997), and *The Triune Creator: A Historical and Systematic Study* (Edinburgh: Edinburgh University Press, 1998). The issue of Trinitarian language of God is helpfully addressed from a feminist perspective by Barbara Brown Zikmund in 'The Trinity and Women's Experience', in *Christian Century* (April 15, 1987), 354–56, and in Janet Martin Soskice, 'Trinity and Feminism', in *The Cambridge Companion to Feminist Theology*, edited by Susan Frank Parsons (Cambridge: Cambridge University Press, 2002), 135–50.

5

SALVATION

In every morning's newspaper we are greeted with news that reflects the enigma of human life. On one page we are told, for example, of the heroic efforts of a man who lost his life while saving a child he did not know but who had been a passenger in a car that had slid off the road into a flooded river. On another page we are told of a man who killed twelve schoolchildren in a wild rampage through a schoolyard and who was then shot dead by police. Turning the page again, we read of a woman who dedicated her life to caring for children who had been abused, who had taken them into her home and loved them as her own children. On the same page there is a story of a village in Ethiopia that is very successful at growing coffee but whose income from what is supplied to global coffee markets is not enough to send the children of the village to school or to provide basic healthcare in their community.

Most of us reading such stories recognise instinctively that something is amiss. We recognise that the heroism of the man who saved the child in danger and the compassion of the woman who devoted her life to caring for those who had suffered abuse reveal humanity as it ought to be, whereas the rampaging gunman and the unjust economic systems of our world are manifestations of the inhumanity that we human beings are capable of. It is not just our daily news, however, that provides evidence of humanity's duplicity.

We can see it in ourselves if we are honest. We have moments of compassion, of generosity, of genuine love for our neighbour, but at other times we behave selfishly, think and speak ill of our neighbour, act in ways that damage others and damage our environment. The signs that something is wrong are evident enough, but what is wrong exactly, and what, if anything, can be done about it?

Christian theology has much to say about this matter. We have encountered already some of the claims that are central to a Christian understanding of our human situation. The world is created by God; it is created for our good; we live under the promise that all the families of the earth will be blessed. These affirmations of faith provide a theological framework within which it is possible to say that the evil that is evident in our world, ranging from a selfish thought to the brutal slaughter of innocent human beings, is a distortion of our true humanity and contradicts the good purposes of God. Among numerous stories told in the Bible that provide a fuller diagnosis of this reality, let us consider three. The first is the story told in Genesis of Adam and Eve and their eating of the fruit of the tree of the knowledge of good and evil. In Genesis 2:15–17, we read:

> The Lord God took the man and put him in the garden of Eden to till it and keep it. And the Lord God commanded the man, 'You may freely eat of every tree of the garden; but of the tree of the knowledge of good and evil you shall not eat, for in the day that you eat of it you shall die.'

The biblical scholar Walter Breuggemann notes three aspects of this passage that shed light on our human condition. There is in the story a vocation, a permission and a prohibition. The man is appointed to the task of nurturing the garden, he is permitted to enjoy the fruits of the garden and he is prohibited from eating the fruit of just one tree. All three are essential to our humanity and yet, as Breuggemann points out, the God depicted here is remembered chiefly as the one who *prohibits* (Breuggemann, *Genesis*, p. 46). That God is commonly remembered as one who places a constraint upon human life is itself a symptom of the disorder that afflicts humankind. It is important to notice, in contrast, that the man is given a great deal of freedom by God: he may *freely* eat from every tree of the garden. There is only one constraint: he shall not eat from the tree of the knowledge of good and evil. Human freedom is portrayed here as a central feature of God's good purpose for humankind, and it remains central, as we shall see, to the account of salvation given in the Bible.

It might seem rather arbitrary and a little extreme to prohibit humanity from eating a piece of fruit and to suggest that the consequences of eating will be death. But stories like this are to be read imaginatively. To eat of the tree of the knowledge of good and evil is, metaphorically speaking, to expose oneself to the reality of evil and so to lose one's innocence. Such exposure will not serve the man well; indeed, it will pose a threat to God's purpose that the creature shall have life, and so, tasting of the tree of the knowledge of good and evil is prohibited by the God who both intends and provides abundantly for humanity's well-being.

The story then proceeds to describe one further provision of God for the man's well-being. God declares that 'it is not good that the man should be alone' (Genesis 2:18). God creates a partner for him, a partner who is bone of his bone and flesh of his flesh (Genesis 2:23). Chapter two closes with a brief account of the intimate union that is established between a man and his wife. Two relationships have thus been established, the relationship between God and humankind, and another between the man and the woman. Having been set in a garden that provides every tree that is 'pleasant to the sight and good for food' (Genesis 2:9), and having been assigned the task of nurturing the garden, the man, now gifted with a companion, is provided with all that he needs to live well. What could possibly go wrong?

What goes wrong is that the human beings begin to suspect that God has been unfair to them, that God has imposed a restriction upon them that robs them of their capacity to reach their full potential. This train of thought emerges in the story through the agency of a serpent, who says to the woman, 'Did God say, "You shall not eat from any tree in the garden"?' (Genesis 3:1). We should not allow ourselves to be distracted by the fact that it was the woman who was tempted first. Some have argued, quite wrongly in my view, that this indicates the weakness of women. Before the story is ended, however, both the man and the woman have succumbed to the temptation that was put before them and both have defied God's instruction. This is not a story about the relative merits or weaknesses of male and female. Nor should we be distracted by the idea of a serpent who speaks. This story is to be read imaginatively. The talking serpent is merely a literary device to introduce the idea of humanity's temptation. The key point is the emergence of the idea that God has been unfair, that he has deprived humanity of some good. Note that the idea of deprivation begins with a distortion of what God actually said. The serpent says, 'Did God say, "You shall not eat from any tree in the garden"?' And the woman replies, 'We may eat of the fruit of the trees in the garden; but God said, "You shall not eat of the fruit of the tree that is in the middle of the garden, nor shall you touch it, or you will die"' (Genesis 3:2–3). The serpent suggests that God had placed a total ban on eating the fruits of the garden, and so plants a seed of discontent in the woman's mind. She recognises, however, that God has not been as restrictive as that, but in her own account of what God has said, she too distorts God's instruction and makes it more restrictive. Not only shall they not eat, they are not even allowed to touch the tree in the middle of the garden. The serpent then continues with his craftiness, saying, 'You will not die; for God knows that when you eat of it your eyes will be opened, and you will be like God … ' (Genesis 3:4–5). Persuaded by this claim and by the beauty of the fruit, the woman takes the fruit and eats it and then shares it with the man. The consequences are that things begin to go badly wrong for these first human beings. They are banished from the garden; they begin to blame others for their wrongdoing; enmity develops between them; pain and suffering ensue, and they must toil to secure food for themselves from the land. The man and the woman are exposed now to the evil and suffering from which God had tried to protect them.

I have suggested earlier that we are dealing in these opening chapters of Genesis with literature that is rather like a parable. Parables are imaginative stories. Their purpose is to reveal the truth of things, often the truth about those to whom the story is told. So it is with this story. At the root of humanity's hardship and suffering and enmity, there is defiance, defiance of God's instruction, and disruption of the relationships that God had established for our good.

A STORY OF TWO SONS

A second story we will consider more briefly. It is a story told by Jesus of a father who had two sons. The younger son says to his father, 'Father, give me the share of the property that will belong to me' (Luke 15:12). We are to imagine here a family who have lived together on the land. Under the benevolent care of the father, they have lived well; there is abundant provision for their needs, and provision, we assume, for succeeding generations. There is an echo here of the scene in the garden of Eden at the beginnings of creation. But the scene is disrupted by the younger son, who wants to divide what is shared between them and go his own way. To claim his inheritance is, in essence, to wish his father dead. The themes apparent here of defiance, of claiming what one imagines to be an entitlement, and of disrupting the relationships that are for one's good echo again the themes of the Genesis story.

The father, not being a coercive father, and respecting the freedom he has given to his children, divides his property between his two sons and allows his younger son to leave. As the story unfolds, we learn that things do not go well for the younger son. He squanders all that he had received from his father and is eventually left destitute, fighting among pigs for scraps of food on the farm where he has managed to get a job. Having sought to be the lord of his own life, the son now finds himself with no life at all. The story then takes an interesting turn. We read:

> But when [the son] came to himself he said, 'How many of my father's hired hands have bread enough and to spare, but here I am dying of hunger! I will get up and go to my father, and I will say to him, "Father, I have sinned against heaven and before you; I am no longer worthy to be called your son; treat me like one of your hired hands."'
>
> (Luke 15:17–19)

What might it mean to suggest that the son 'came to himself'? The phrase implies, first of all, that in his state of destitution and apart from his father, the son was not himself. His identity had been undermined. He was no longer the human being that he was created to be. 'Coming to himself' means that the son recalls his true identity. He remembers his father's house, the benefits of sonship that he has squandered, and the relationship that he has given up. The story, like the account of Adam and Eve in the garden of Eden, is offering a diagnosis of our human situation. At the root of human suffering and the loss of our humanity, and at the root of the world's disorder, lies a decision to go our own way, to become lords of our own lives in defiance of the relationships for which we were made.

So the son decides to return to his father. It would be presumptuous, he supposes, to be treated again as a son, and so he plans to ask his father if he can be treated like one of the father's servants. Even that proximity to his father would be far better than the non-life that he lives now.

> So he set off and went to his father. But while he was still far off, his father saw him and was filled with compassion; he ran and put his arms around him and kissed him. Then the son said to him, 'Father, I have sinned against heaven and before you; I am no longer worthy to be called your son.' But the father said to his slaves, 'Quickly, bring out a robe – the best one – and put it on him; put a ring on his finger and sandals on his feet. And get the fatted calf and kill it, and let us eat and celebrate; for this son of mine was dead and is alive again; he was lost and is found!' And they began to celebrate.
>
> (Luke 15:20–24)

This homecoming is not what the son had expected. He does not get what he deserves. Instead, he is reinstated immediately to the position of sonship, beginning with the compassionate embrace of his father, who had waited and watched for his son's return all the days that he had been away. The robe and the ring and the sandals are all signs of the father's provision lavished abundantly on his beloved son who was lost and now is found, who was dead but is now alive again.

The theological term applied to this homecoming is 'salvation'. The meaning of the term is very broad. As we will see, it is a term that applies ultimately to the whole of creation perfected and reconciled to God, but at its heart, salvation means the restoration of right relationship, the overcoming of sin and death, and the recovery of true identity.

There is one further act in this drama. The older brother who was working out in the fields, as he had done faithfully year after year, hears the commotion and goes to the father's house to find out what is going on. On learning that his younger brother has returned and that his father has spared no expense in welcoming his brother home, the older son becomes angry and complains to his father that for all the years that he had worked, he had never enjoyed the abundance now lavished on his wayward brother. The older son supposes that people should get their just deserts. But salvation does not work that way. Salvation, according to the biblical story, comes about through the overflowing of God's love. The father in Jesus' parable reveals the love and the character of God. Love has no interest in keeping scores and rewarding people according to what they deserve. That is the good news of the gospel. When God has his way and salvation happens, people do not get what they deserve, but vastly more. And so the father gently reminds his older son, 'Son, you are always with me, and all that is mine is yours' (Luke 15:31). The fruits of salvation have been his all along. The tragedy of the older son was not that he had been denied but that he had failed to recognise the abundance of his father's blessing.

We might get the impression sometimes, when dipping into the vast library of theological books, that theology is always a matter of complex and learned propositions. But these two biblical stories that we have considered are theology at its most profound. They reveal truly how things are in God's world. They reveal the reality of the world's disorder and the part humanity plays in bringing that disorder about. They reveal our defiance of God, our determination to go it alone, and the disruption of our true identity brought about through human sin. As is captured so powerfully in the parable of the prodigal son, the biblical story as a whole reveals also that despite our human waywardness, God's love for us is unwavering. God's intention for us is that we should 'come to ourselves' and take up our true identity as beloved children of God.

THE CROSS OF JESUS CHRIST

The two stories we have considered so far reveal crucial dimensions of our human situation. We are made to live in communion with God and with one another, and all that is needed for our well-being has been provided for us by God. But humanity acts in defiance of that divine intent and blessing. We attempt to go it alone, but precisely in doing so, the good order of God's world is disrupted and we are plunged into a chaos that robs us of our true identity. Despite the profundity of these two stories, however, they do not yet reveal the full extent of humanity's defiance of God, nor the greatest depths to which sinful humanity may sink. It is not in a parable that the depths of sinfulness are most starkly revealed, but in the grim realities of human history. Every age provides instances of human evil. In our own time, we may think of the brutal massacre of villagers in northern Nigeria, the rape of a teenage girl by a gang of men who finish their work by leaving her dead, a bomb planted in a busy street or dropped from a plane overhead that tears human lives to shreds.

Where is God in all of this? And what salvation can there be from such brutality? The Christian answer is that God is in the midst of it. In the person of Christ, God enters into the midst of human suffering and evil, takes it upon himself, and suffers its worst consequences. The Christian answer to the question of God's whereabouts in the face of human suffering and evil is heard on the lips of a centurion who was standing guard at Jesus' crucifixion. On seeing Jesus die, the centurion confessed, 'Truly this man was God's Son!' (Mark 15:39). Crucifixion is a brutal punishment. Nails are driven through the hands and feet of a victim strung up on a cross. With the full weight of his body hanging from the nails, the victim is left to die. The centurion's declaration, if it is true, entails that God does not remain remote from human suffering or from the brutal reality of human sin. In the crucifixion of Jesus, God takes it upon himself and suffers its full consequences through to the point of death.

The first sign in the gospels of Jesus' willingness to take the burden of human sin upon himself is his baptism in the river Jordan. John the Baptist was an itinerant Jewish preacher who called people to repentance and offered baptism as a sign of their acceptance of the forgiveness of sin. On hearing John's preaching and his call to repentance, Jesus submitted himself to be baptised by John. John himself recognises the inappropriateness of this (see Matthew 3:14). After all, Jesus is described in the book of Hebrews as being 'without sin' (Hebrews 4:15). He had no need of baptism for himself. And yet, in submitting himself to John's baptism, Jesus takes responsibility for our human situation. He takes our need for repentance and forgiveness upon himself. He shoulders the burden of our sin. That is a decision that will take him eventually to the cross, where he encounters human sin and evil at its worst. Although, as was apparent in the stories of the temptation in the garden and the parable of the prodigal son, sin and evil are rooted in humanity's rejection of God's good purposes for his creation, God does not angrily reject humanity nor stand aloof from our sinfulness. Rather God enters into the midst of it in order to rescue us from the consequences of our sin.

It is in this light that we can begin to understand what takes place on the cross. In crucifying the beloved Son of God, who had come among us declaring good news for the poor, release for the captives, recovery of sight for the blind and freedom for the oppressed (see Luke 4:16–21), humanity's defiance of God takes its most extreme form. Jesus' proclamation of God's good purposes for humanity are met with the demand to 'Crucify him!'

According to the gospel writers, Jesus saw this coming and could have avoided it. He could have steered clear of Jerusalem; he could have avoided upsetting the political and religious authorities of the day; he could have retreated to his hometown in Galilee and abandoned his mission to declare God's call upon humanity to live in covenant relationship with him. That Jesus chose not to avoid the defiant reaction and the violent rejection is an expression of the steadfast love that God has for his people. The crucifixion reveals at once the depths to which sinful humanity may sink and the glory of the God who will not abandon his covenant commitment to us even when we do our worst. Despite his anguish at the prospect of death, evident especially in the account of Jesus in the garden of Gethsemane, Jesus goes through with it (see Matthew 29:36–46; Mark 14:32–42; Luke 22:39–46). He remains steadfast in the commitment expressed at his baptism to take the consequences of human sinfulness upon himself. The cross reveals that humanity's defiance of God ends in death. But it is at this point that everything gets turned upside down. What is rightfully ours is suffered by God. The one who is without sin bears the full brunt of our defiance and suffers in our place. To put it in the common language of Christian confession, Christ dies for our sins.

There is a spiritual originally sung by black slaves in America who saw in Christ the possibility of salvation. The slaves sang,

> Were you there when they crucified my Lord?
> Were you there when they crucified my Lord?
> O! Sometimes it causes me to tremble! tremble! tremble!
> Were you there when they crucified my Lord?

There are several aspects of the crucifixion of Jesus that might cause the onlooker to tremble. There is of course the horror of crucifixion itself. Well might one tremble in the face of human brutality. One might tremble as well with the centurion who recognised that the one who suffers here is the beloved Son of God. And finally, one might tremble at the truth revealed here, the truth that Christ dies in our place. The words of the spiritual suggest also, perhaps, that there are depths to the workings of love that cannot be comprehended through reasoned explanation. There are realities in the face of which we can only stand in awe.

That reticence to explain what takes place on the cross of Jesus Christ is reflected in the church's refusal ever to sanction a single account of how it is that the death of Christ brings about salvation. While the church has produced definitive creedal statements about Jesus' identity as truly divine and truly human, and while it has made definitive claims about the Triune being of God, when it comes to the confession that Jesus died for our sins, the church has resisted any singular explanation of the mystery. It has offered instead, beginning in the New Testament itself, a number of metaphors that offer partial explanations of how it is that Christ's death atones for our sin. Christ's death is spoken of, for example, as a ransom that sets humanity free from its captivity to sin, as a sacrifice that atones for our sin, as a victory over the forces of sin and evil, as a penalty paid for sin and as a moral example of self-sacrificing love. A thin strand in church tradition has also spoken of Christ's death as comparable to that of a woman who dies in travail while bringing to birth a new creation. A full consideration of each of these metaphors lies beyond the scope of this book, but each is considered briefly in what follows.

> Atonement is a term often used to speak of the overcoming of human sin and the re-establishment of communion with God.

A RANSOM FOR SIN

The idea of Christ's death as a ransom has its origins in a verse appearing in both Mark's and Matthew's gospels – 'For the Son of

Man came not to be served but to serve, and to give his life as a ransom for many' (Mark 10:45; Matthew 20:28) – and in a similar reference in 1 Timothy 2:6. The idea that Christ gave himself as a ransom for many (or for all) was quoted frequently in the early church but was first developed as a theory of the atonement by Origen (c.185–c.254) Origen asked to whom was the ransom paid, and offers his own suggestion that the ransom of Christ's life (or soul) was paid to the devil, who had taken humanity captive. Christ gives his own life to free humanity from the clutches of death but then outwits the devil, by rising from the dead and proving that he is stronger than death. A similar idea appears in the theology of Gregory of Nyssa, who writes, 'The Enemy, therefore, beholding in [Jesus] such power, saw also in Him an opportunity for an advance, in the exchange, upon the value of what he held. For this reason he chooses Him as a ransom for those who were shut up in the prison of death' (Gregory of Nyssa, 'The Great Catechism', ch. 23). Other theologians of the early church, however, among them Gregory Nazianzus (c.330–89) and, later, Anselm of Canterbury (1033–1109), expressed reservations about the idea that God would pay a ransom to the devil. The metaphor of ransom points to the fact that the death of Christ secures the release of sinners from bondage, but metaphorical speech often serves to highlight one feature of a particular reality and should not be pushed to explain the whole matter. Accordingly, Gregory Nazianzus and Anselm both thought it unnecessary to ask to whom the ransom was paid.

SACRIFICE

A second metaphor prominent in Christian reflection upon the death of Christ is the metaphor of sacrifice. The language here is drawn from the Old Testament and from wider traditions of religious sacrifice. There are various forms of sacrifice referred to in the Old Testament, the most relevant of which is the sacrifice made once a year on the Day of Atonement, when the high priest of Israel enters into the holy of holies in the Temple, offers the blood of various animals on the altar and so makes atonement for the sins of the people. The Old Testament offers no straightforward explanation, however, of how the practice of sacrifice is thought to be effective in overcoming sin. Perhaps the value of the ritual of sacrifice lies in its symbolic power rather than in a strictly logical account of how sin is overcome. The sacrifice of an animal serves as a reminder of the seriousness of sin, and of its deathly consequences, while the blood offered on the altar reminds us that all created life is owed to God and should be returned to him. Jewish tradition specifies that on the Day of Atonement, Jews should refrain from all work. They should also abstain from eating or drinking, wearing leather shoes, bathing or washing, anointing themselves with perfume and indulging in sexual relations. The day should be given over to repentance, and so the specified practices and pleasures should be given up. Those who participate in the rituals are reminded that reconciliation and atonement involves sacrifice, rather than carrying on as they did before.

Some of these symbolic elements were thought by the New Testament writers to transfer readily to the atoning death of Christ. As the Christian tradition developed further, however, the sacrificial death of Christ was sometimes regarded as a means of appeasing an angry God. There are antecedents for this view in the Old Testament idea of propitiatory sacrifices, but the idea of an angry God who needs to be placated and who considers the shedding of blood to be a suitable satisfaction takes us some distance from what Jesus himself reveals to us of God's character, and indeed from the Old Testament's own expression of God's impatience with such notions. In Isaiah, for instance, we read:

> What to me is the multitude of your sacrifices? Says the Lord;
> I have had enough of burnt offerings of rams and the fat of fed beasts;
> I do not delight in the blood of bulls, or of lambs, or of goats.
>
> (Isaiah 1:11)

Hosea 6:6 takes up a similar theme: 'For I desire steadfast love not sacrifice, the knowledge of God rather than burnt offerings.' And Micah, in 6:7–8, recognises that the Lord does not require the traditional sacrifices but requires instead that he does justice, loves kindness and walks humbly with his God.

To speak, then, of Jesus' death as a sacrifice atoning for sin cannot mean that an angry God is appeased by the shedding of blood. It may serve as a reminder of the costliness of sin; it may serve to remind us that defiance of the God who gives life results ultimately in death; it may serve as a reminder that we cannot have salvation without giving up the sinful practices in which we now indulge. But to speak of Christ's death as a sacrifice draws attention, above all, to what God gives up for us – his own beloved Son. The Father lets the Son go, into the realm of sin and death, in order to rescue those who have strayed there, and in order to proclaim to them the news that the Father wants them home. The Father lets the Son go, even though he knows that the mission of the Son will be met initially by further defiance and by a further exercise of humanity's determination to rid itself of God. The Father lets the Son go, and in response, the Son, in full agreement with the Father's purpose, gives up his own life so that humankind in its sinfulness will not be left bereft of God. To speak in this way of the Father 'letting the Son go' echoes the parable of the prodigal son considered earlier. The allusion to the parable reminds us that Jesus really does take upon himself the prodigal sinfulness of wayward humanity. An especially powerful exposition of the drama of salvation is provided in Karl Barth's discussion of 'The Way of the Son of God into the Far Country' (see Barth, *Church Dogmatics*, vol. IV.1, pp. 157–210).

The language of sacrifice is again suggestive and evocative rather than exhaustively descriptive. It doesn't capture the full reality of the cross, but, within the limitations of human speech, it gives an inkling of what God has done for us.

THE CROSS AS VICTORY

Another metaphor that has been used quite frequently in the tradition to speak of Christ's work on the cross is the metaphor of victory. In this view, advocated in the twentieth century especially by Gustav Aulen (1879–1978), Christ is portrayed as doing battle against the forces of evil in the world and winning victory over them. Colossians 2:15 is often cited in support of this view: 'He disarmed the rulers and authorities and made a public example of them, triumphing over them in it.' John 12:30–33 is also appealed to: 'Jesus answered ... "Now is the judgement of this world; now the ruler of this world will be driven out. And I, when I am lifted up from the earth, I will draw all people to myself." He said this to indicate the kind of death he was to die.' The victory over evil takes place not just through the cross, however, but throughout the life, death and resurrection of Jesus. Already in his ministry, Jesus is portrayed in the gospels as casting out demons, rebuking the devil and overcoming powers that are hostile to God. In the cross and resurrection, however, the victory is made complete. The forces of death cannot hold Jesus, and through his victory over them the world itself is set free. It is important to note Aulen's insistence that this is an 'objective' view of the atonement, by which he means that the victory is accomplished irrespective of its subjective appropriation by individuals. The devil has been defeated whether we recognise and accept it or not. An important point of discussion in all accounts of the atonement is whether the work of Christ in overcoming sin and death is complete and effectual for the world apart from individual acceptance of that reality, or whether it requires to be appropriated subjectively through faith in order to take effect. Defenders of particular accounts of the atonement will often argue that there is both an objective and a necessary subjective element to the efficacy of Christ's work.

Although Aulen's claim that Christ's saving work was understood in the early church predominantly in terms of victory has been contested in recent scholarship, the language of victory associated with Jesus' life, death and resurrection does certainly appear in the New Testament witness and does feature in the theological reflections of the patristic theologians. The point at issue is whether it is justifiable to claim that this is the 'classic' or dominant idea of the atonement. That matter cannot be settled here, but before passing on from the idea of Christ securing victory over the powers of sin and death, it is worth noting Colin Gunton's point that if the cross is to be understood as a victory, then it casts a whole new light on what true victory involves (see Gunton, *The Actuality of Atonement*, pp. 53–82).

We are used to victories being won in battle through the exercise of superior force and through the subjection and humiliation of one's enemies. But, if it is appropriate to speak of the work of Christ on the cross as a victory, then it will only be as we come to a new understanding of the nature of victory. There were those who were standing by the cross who mocked Jesus, saying, 'He saved others; he cannot save himself. He is the King of Israel; let him come down from the cross now, and we will believe in him' (Matthew 27:42; cf. Luke 23:35; Mark 15:31). Such actions would, in the eyes of the world, have constituted a victory for Jesus. His tormentors would have been made to look foolish, and death would have been avoided. But what would such a victory have meant? I suggest it would mean that the ways of this world represent, after all, the truth about the world. It would mean that ugly force must be confronted by the exercise of superior power. It would mean that saving one's own life is what really matters in the end. It would mean that victory involves the humiliation of one's opponents. But Jesus does none of these things. He bears the suffering inflicted upon him and, according to the account in Luke's gospel, prays, 'Father forgive them, for they do not know what they are doing' (Luke 23:34).

What we see here is a re-shaping of what victory itself might mean. In the light of the cross, a new understanding of victory is disclosed, an understanding taken up, for example, by Paul, who writes, 'Bless those who persecute you; bless and do not curse them', and further, ' ... if your enemies are hungry, feed them; if they are thirsty, give them something to drink ... ' (Romans 12:14, 20). To confess that Christ is victorious over the forces of evil is to recognise that true victory is accomplished not through brute force and the angry suppression of one's enemies, but rather through forgiveness and the power of love.

A PENALTY PAID FOR SIN?

It has been common in Christian tradition to confess that Christ has paid the penalty for our sin. This way of speaking about the cross is variously classified as the Latin theory, the Anselmian theory, the satisfaction theory, and the penal substitution theory, from which we may gather that it has its roots in the Latin, rather than the Greek, fathers, that it received its most systematic formulation in the writings of St Anselm and that it places heavy emphasis on the notions of justice and retribution. While a number of variations on this theme have emerged in the theological tradition, the underlying assumption is that sin incurs a debt and this debt must be paid. The question of how the debt is to be paid has elicited varying responses. At one end of the spectrum, it is argued that the debt is paid through Christ's bearing of the punishment due to us, thereby appeasing the wrath of God. This view is sometimes accompanied by the insistence that those who do not accept what Christ has done for them will suffer eternally in hell. God is portrayed here as an angry and vengeful God, somewhat removed, it might be suggested, from the God made known through Jesus. At the other end of the spectrum, it has been proposed by such as the Scottish theologian John McLeod Campbell (1800–1872) that atonement is accomplished through Christ's offering on our behalf the perfect life of loving obedience to the Father and repentance for the sin of humankind. Punishment plays no role in Campbell's account of how God's justice is satisfied. The love and the grace of God is the dominant theme, rather than God's fiery anger.

It has often been argued that the idea of Christ suffering punishment on our behalf emerged relatively late in Christian tradition, and solely in Western Christianity rather than among Eastern Orthodox Christians. To begin with, the biblical verses usually appealed to in support of penal substitution are, at best, ambiguous concerning the question of whether Christ was punished. Isaiah 53:4–11 seems to come closest to an explicit suggestion that the 'servant of Yahweh' is in fact punished by God, but New Testament verses suggesting that Christ 'bore our sin' (1 Peter 2:24), that he died for sins (1 Peter 3:18), that he became a curse for us (Galatians 3:13) or was made sin for us (2 Corinthians 5:21) do not mention punishment explicitly and can certainly be interpreted in other ways. Nor is the suggestion that Christ was *punished* for our sins prevalent in the early church. An exception occurs in Augustine, who writes, 'Christ, though guiltless, took our punishment, that He might cancel our guilt, and do away with our punishment' (Augustine, *Reply to Faustus the Manichaean*, XIV.4). Note, however, that Augustine elsewhere denies that Christ's death was necessary to appease the Father (Augustine, *On the Holy Trinity*, XI.15).

Although the notion of Christ being punished for our sins is rare in the early church, the idea that something must be offered to God in order to pay the price of sin appears more frequently. For Tertullian, forgiveness of our sin does not come free of charge. The price to be paid is a true repentance. ' ... how inconsistent is it', he writes, 'to expect pardon of sins (to be granted) to a repentance which they have not fulfilled! This is to hold out your hand for merchandise, but not produce the price' (Tertullian, *On Repentance*, VI). Genuine repentance, Tertullian continues, will be apparent in a changed life, one characterised by meritorious acts such as fasting, voluntary celibacy and martyrdom. A generation after Tertullian, Cyprian of Carthage (c.200–258) argued that the surplus of merit that could be built up by the individual had been achieved in sufficient measure for all people in the life and death of Jesus Christ. This merit, built up by Christ, is paid to God as satisfaction or compensation for human sin.

It was Anselm of Canterbury who developed the idea of satisfaction into a comprehensive theory of atonement. In answer to the question 'Why did God become man?' Anselm proposed that Christ came to restore order to the universe, an order that had been disrupted by human sin. If human sin were to go unpunished, then the universe would be an unjust and irrational place and the God responsible for its creation would no longer be worthy to be called God. The point, however, is not that God demands satisfaction for sin because God in some way needs to be appeased. What is at stake is the order and the goodness of creation, and so also the honour of the God who is responsible for it. Anselm writes,

> If Divine Wisdom did not restore balance when perversity attempts to disturb the regular order of things, there would be caused in that universe, which God should rule, a certain deformity from this violated symmetry of its order, and God would fail in his government.
>
> (Anselm, *Cur Deus Homo*, I.xv)

Because of human sin, the universe has been disrupted in ways that cannot be ignored by a God who is both just and good. To re-establish justice in the universe and to overcome the estrangement caused by sin, some compensation must be made, but, precisely on account of its sin, humanity cannot make any such compensation. It cannot pay the debt that it has incurred.

According to Anselm, God takes responsibility himself for the payment of the debt. This is why 'God becomes man'. God provides humanity with the gift of the Son who, acting on behalf of all humanity, takes death upon himself, thus paying the price that justice requires. This perfect human life, when given freely as a gift to God, outweighs in value the whole of human sin and makes amends for humanity's disruption of the relationship with God. The debt is paid and the burden of guilt is removed from around humanity's neck. The emphasis in Anselm is on the unmerited gift of grace by which God in person bears the consequences of human sin. It is not the angry but the merciful God who offers to humankind his own Son to stand in the place that we should stand and to take our death upon himself. This setting right of the relationship involves, therefore, not only the overcoming of sin but also the glorification of God, whose purposes are thereby brought to fulfilment.

Anselm's account of the atonement encourages us to consider what divine justice consists in. It is often assumed that justice is done when perpetrators of wrongdoing get their just deserts, when, in other words, they are made to pay for their crime through the imposition of some punishment. But Anselm's account of divine justice suggests an altogether different goal, the goal of restoring order and right relationship. Justice is done when God's good ordering of things is restored. It is this idea that lies at the heart of the biblical concept of justification. The justification of sinners does not mean that their sinful actions turn out to be justified after all. It means, rather, that through incorporation into Christ they are restored to right relationship with God following the disruption of that relationship caused by human sin. Similarly, the biblical claim that they are made righteous also refers to their being restored to right relationship with God. There are moral implications that flow from this 'right relationship' but, understood in biblical terms, righteousness is, first and foremost, a gift of divine grace. It is not a status achieved through our own moral prowess. This reality was expressed in the theology of Martin Luther, who spoke of the righteousness attained through Christ as 'imputed righteousness'. Luther, along with other Protestant Reformers, emphasised that the righteousness attained through justification is given freely by God and is not earned through any merit of our own.

Luther thus made a distinction between *justification* (the external act by which God declares the sinner to be righteous) and *sanctification* or *regeneration* (the internal process of renewal within the individual). Although the two are treated as inseparable, they are nevertheless to be distinguished. It is this distinction that gives rise to Luther's famous phrase that the person of faith is *simul iustus et peccator,* at once justified and yet a sinner. The relationship with God has been put right. Sinners have been justified even though it is true that they go on sinning. Sanctification, accordingly, is the ongoing process of being made holy and is not finally completed until the final reconciliation of all things in Christ. Not all have agreed with Luther's account. Another major Reformer, John Calvin, believed that sanctification of the sinner took place at the same time as justification. Just as the sinner is justified in Christ, so they are declared to be holy in virtue of their incorporation into the life of Christ.

A word might be said here also about what divine judgement consists in. It is a common and very unfortunate mistake to suppose that judgement necessarily entails punishment. Properly speaking, judgement simply means to lay bare the truth of things. In this sense, the cross of Christ certainly constitutes a divine judgement on human sin. It lays bare the terrible reality of sin and where it leads. There can be no doubting, in the light of Christ's death, that the consequences of our defiance of God are very serious indeed. Sin ends in death and in Godforsakenness. But in this same event of divine judgement the great depths of God's mercy are revealed. Far from being punished, the sinful creature is spared. What is more, in Christ's resurrection from the dead, death itself is defeated. It is robbed of its power to separate us from God. Through this execution of divine justice, God's gift of life for the creature and God's right ordering of things are restored.

A MORAL EXAMPLE

A good number of theologians over the years have drawn attention to the importance of the example set by Christ in giving himself utterly to the cause of love. He fulfilled in his own life the sum of the law, which is to love God and to love one's neighbour as oneself (see Matthew 22:36–40). The ultimate expression of this love for neighbour is the willingness to lay down one's life for them (cf. John 15:13). Some theologians have taken these words of Jesus as a clue to understanding how his death might be seen as a death 'for us'. It provides for us an example of selfless love that we are called to follow and so leave behind the self-serving ways of sin. This account of atonement is commonly attributed to the medieval philosopher and theologian Peter Abelard (1079–1142), although it is by no means unique to him. Abelard did not propose that the exemplary value of Christ's death was all there was to it – he made use also of the sacrificial account of Christ's overcoming of sin – but he was deeply impressed by the impact upon us of Christ's example that kindles in our hearts a 'true charity [that] should not now shrink from doing anything for him' (Abelard, 'Exposition of the Epistle to the Romans II', on Romans 3:19–26). It is important to point out that Abelard was no Pelagian; he did not suppose that we have it in our own power to fulfil the command of love as Christ himself did. Rather, the capacity to love is 'a gift of divine grace' that frees us from our slavery to sin.

> The term 'Pelagian' refers to the idea that we have the capacity to become righteous ourselves apart from divine grace. This view takes its name from Pelagius, a fourth-century monk who advocated such a view.

The idea that the principal value of Christ's life and death rests in the moral example it sets for us became very popular in the nineteenth century, partly under the influence of the philosopher Immanuel Kant (1724–1804). Kant had a very high estimation of our capacity both to discover the content of the moral law and to fulfil it. 'Christ' functioned in Kant's scheme as an archetype of the morally perfect human being who may or may not have existed, but whether he did or he didn't exist, humanity is certainly capable of conceiving this idea of moral perfection for itself and so does not really need the example of Christ. Theological admirers of Kant in the nineteenth century sought to 'Christianise' Kant's ideas and argued that Christ really was necessary to provide us with an exemplar of the truly moral life. This has become a standard position of liberal theology, which typically conceives the saving significance of Christ in terms of the example he sets of compassionate service to our neighbour, the execution of justice, the formation of inclusive community and so on. While there can be no doubting Christ's call upon us to live compassionate and upright lives, or the biblical injunction to do justice and to love mercy, many Christians, in contrast with the exemplarist view, regard the cross of Christ as the means by which God brings about a salvation that we cannot accomplish for ourselves.

THE TRAVAIL OF GOD

Prompted by the work of feminist theologians in recent years, the Christian community is becoming more aware of the feminine and maternal imagery sometimes used of God in the Bible. Drawing upon such imagery, the idea of Jesus' death as the travail of God, and of Jesus himself as acting like a mother who dies in childbirth, may well illumine for the church important aspects of that event which it confesses to be at the heart of its faith. This suggestion appears in the work of Julian of Norwich (1342–1416), who writes:

> We know that all our mothers' bearing is [bearing of] us to pain and to dying; and what is this but that our Very Mother, Jesus, He – All-Love – beareth us to joy and to endless living? – blessed may be he! Thus he sustaineth us within Himself in love; and travailed, unto the full time that He would suffer the sharpest throes and the most grievous pains that ever were or ever shall be; and died at the last.
>
> (Julian of Norwich, *Revelations of Divine Love*, LX)

Before Julian, Anselm of Canterbury in his Prayer to St Paul had also compared Christ's suffering to a mother in travail:

> For, longing to bear sons into life,
> you tasted of death,
> and by dying you begot them.
> You did this in your own self,
> your servants by your commands and help.
> You as the author, they as the ministers.
> So you, Lord God, are the great mother.
>
> (Anselm, prayer 10, *The Prayers and Meditations of St Anselm*, 153–54)

To quote one more source, Marguerite of Oingt (c.1240–1310) writes:

> Ah, my sweet and lovely Lord, with what love you have labored for me and bore me through your whole life. But when the time approached for you to be delivered, your labor pains were so great that your holy sweat was like great drops of blood that came out from your body and fell on the earth ... Ah! Sweet Lord Jesus Christ, who ever saw a mother suffer

such a birth! For when the hour of your delivery came you were placed on the hard bed of the cross ... and your nerves and all your veins were broken. And truly it is no surprise that your veins burst when in one day you gave birth to the whole world.

(Marguerite of Oingt, *Pagina meditationum*, chapters 30–39, cited in Bynum, *Jesus as Mother*, p. 153)

There are biblical precedents for this manner of speaking. Deuteronomy 32:18–19, for example, alleges that 'you the people of Israel have forgotten the God who gave you birth', while in Isaiah 42:14–16, God declares that he will cry out like a woman in travail. Among a number of passages in the New Testament that use similar language, we may note in particular the well-known dialogue of Jesus with Nicodemus, in which Jesus advises that 'no one can see the kingdom of God without being born from above' [or, without being born anew] (John 3:3). When Nicodemus enquires how such a new birth might be possible, he receives the answer, eventually, that new life will come about when the Son of Man is 'lifted up' (John 3:14). That this is a reference to the cross is made explicit in chapter 12 of the gospel, where Jesus is reported to have said: 'And I, when I am lifted up from the earth will draw all people to myself.' John adds the explanatory note: 'He said this to indicate the kind of death he was to die' (John 12:32–33). Jesus is to be understood as the one who dies in order that we might be born to eternal life. It is by virtue of his death that we may be called 'children of God'. It is Christ who labours that we might receive new life, so that 'all who receive him, who believe in his name, he gives power to become children of God, who are born, not of blood nor of the will of the flesh nor of human will, but *of God*' (John 1:12–13).

As we have seen earlier, the ultimate tragedy of sin is that it destroys life. Sin is defeated, therefore, not when it is punished but when new life is given. The metaphor of travail draws attention to the fact that this new life comes about through the suffering of Christ on the cross. He it is who gives birth to a new creation.

RESURRECTION

I have focused above, as the metaphors of atonement themselves tend to do, on the cross of Christ, but the full story of Christ's saving work must refer to his journey through human birth, through life and death, through resurrection and ascension, and to his giving of the Spirit through whose enlivening power humanity is drawn to participate in the new life that Christ has made possible. We will have more to say of this in the following two chapters.

Before concluding this chapter, however, attention must be paid to the resurrection of Jesus from the dead. The cross is no victory over sin and evil without the resurrection, and it cannot be said to pave the way to new life if Christ himself is defeated by death. Nor even does Christ's death hold much value as a moral example if in the end the moral life is snuffed out and the forces of evil win the day. The gospels tell the story of Christ's life and death because in the end Jesus was raised. That is what makes his journey through life and through death the world-changing event that it is.

We live in an age that is inclined to be sceptical about the claim that Jesus was raised by God from death. Aside from outright denial of the resurrection, that scepticism manifests itself in the claim often heard that the resurrection is a mythical way of speaking about the continuing influence of Christ or of the rise of faith in the hearts and minds of those who follow him. These explanations claim considerably less, however, than the New Testament itself does. However hard it may be to grasp, the news declared by the first Christians is that the one who was crucified was raised by God, left the tomb empty, appeared among them in the flesh, shared food with them and revealed to them the wounds of his crucifixion (see, e.g., John 20:24–29). This overcoming of death through the raising of Jesus from the dead is an event that parallels God's creation of life in the beginning and is, in fact, the inauguration of a new creation. Theologians often speak of the resurrection as an eschatological event. It reveals in the midst of history the shape of God's future, in which God's promise of abundant life will be realised in its fullness.

Precisely for this reason, the resurrection cannot be accommodated within our customary views of what is possible in this world. We suppose, on the basis of good evidence, that dead people are not raised to life. We make that judgement, however, on the basis of what we commonly see in history. To speak of the resurrection as an eschatological event, however, is to say that its true content and reality is determined, not by all that has happened in the past, but by what God will bring to fruition in the future.

The resurrection is a foretaste of what is to come, rather than an effect of all that has gone before. That is why historians cannot finally prove one way or the other whether the resurrection happened or not. Its full reality is accessible only through faith, only by trusting oneself to the promise of God. The same is true of salvation. The reality of new life in Christ, a life shaped by God's promised future rather than by the sin of the past, can be grasped only by those who have begun to live that life, who have taken the first steps of discipleship and who have discovered in doing so that the one who calls them forward to new life is, as John's gospel puts it, the way, the truth and the life (John 14:6).

FOR FURTHER READING

On the metaphors of atonement, see Colin E. Gunton, *The Actuality of Atonement* (Edinburgh: T&T Clark, 1988), and Gustav Aulen, *Christus Victor* (New York: Macmillan, 1931). Further accounts of the atonement may be found in Tom Smail, *Once and for All: A Confession of the Cross* (London: Darton, Longman & Todd, 1998), Linda D. Peacore, *The Role of Women's Experience in Feminist Theologies of the Atonement* (Eugene, OR: Pickwick Publications, 2010) and Paul Fiddes, 'Salvation', in *The Oxford Handbook of Systematic Theology*, edited by John Webster, Kathryn Tanner and Iain Torrance (Oxford: Oxford University Press, 2007), 176–96. A more extensive treatment is offered in Thomas F. Torrance's book *Atonement: The Person and Work of Christ* (Downers Grove, IL: InterVarsity Press, 2009). The idea of the travail of God is more extensively discussed in Murray Rae, 'The Travail of God', *International Journal of Systematic Theology* 5.1 (March 2003), 47–61. A selection of readings on the work of Christ spanning Christian tradition from Irenaeus to Rosemary Radford Ruether may be found in Lindsey Hall, Murray Rae and Steve Holmes, eds., *Christian Doctrine: A Reader* (London: SCM Press, 2010). The perspectives of liberation theologians are helpfully discussed in Theo Witvliet, *The Way of the Black Messiah* (London: SCM Press, 1987).

6

CHRISTIAN HOPE

The preceding chapter on sin and salvation has a strong focus on the overcoming of human sin and evil. The overcoming of humanity's sinful defiance of God is an important feature of the biblical story, but the vision of salvation provided in the Bible is much broader in scope than has so far been suggested. In fact, God's creative and redemptive purposes for the world encompass the whole of creation. Some accounts of salvation offered by Christians suggest that salvation is entirely a matter of what happens to the individual human soul after death, but this view falsely supposes that our bodies are not an essential feature of our humanity, devalues the creation that God has made and can be sustained only through a very selective reading of the Bible. That God's purposes of salvation encompass the whole of the created world is indicated in the biblical concept of the kingdom of God, and even more so in the biblical vision of a new creation or a new heaven and a new earth. These biblical concepts suggest that God's good purposes for the world involve a great deal more than the fate of the individual human soul after death.

A fuller appreciation of the scope of salvation as presented in Scripture takes us to that part of Christian theology known as eschatology. Eschatology is a word that is derived from the Greek word *eschatos*, meaning the end, or the last things. Eschatology is the study of the last things and of the end to which all things are directed by God. Put otherwise, we may say that eschatology is that branch of theology that seeks to investigate and articulate the Christian hope.

Despite this future orientation, however, many theologians have argued that eschatology is not concerned only with the future. It is concerned as well with the impact that God's coming future has or ought to have on our present existence. In the teaching of Jesus, for example, we hear a great deal about the coming kingdom of God, but Jesus suggests that the kingdom is not merely a future reality; it has 'come near' in and through his own ministry. Furthermore, things are different now, because of the coming of God's kingdom. According to Mark's gospel, 'Jesus came to Galilee, proclaiming the good news of God, and saying, "The time is fulfilled, and the kingdom of God has come near; repent, and believe in the good news"' (Mark 1:14–15; cf. Matthew 3:2, 4:17). Jesus here indicates the closeness of the kingdom of God but is not clear about whether it is already present. This ambiguity is found in much of Jesus' teaching about the kingdom of God, although there are times, such as in Luke 17:21, when Jesus says more explicitly that the kingdom of God is already 'among you'. This ambiguity in Jesus' teaching about the kingdom has generally led to theologians adopting one of three positions. Some, like the influential German theologian and missionary doctor Albert Schweitzer (1875–1965), suggest that the kingdom of God is entirely a future reality. It has not yet begun. Others, such as the English New Testament scholar C. H. Dodd (1884–1973), emphasise the present reality of the kingdom brought about through the ministry of Jesus. This view is known as *realised* eschatology. A third view, advocated by the German New Testament scholar Joachim Jeremias (1900–79), is that the kingdom of God has been inaugurated through the ministry of Jesus – it has begun, but it is not yet completed. Its full realisation lies in the future.

A second set of questions arising in this sphere of theological enquiry concerns the interpretation of the biblical anticipation of a new heaven and a new earth, found in the Old Testament book of Isaiah (65:17 and 66:22) and again in the New Testament, particularly in Revelation 21:1, where we read 'Then I saw a new heaven and a new earth; for the first heaven and the first earth had passed away, and the sea was no more.' The scope of God's saving work here extends beyond humanity to the whole creation, but are we to understand this biblical hope for a new heaven and a new earth as a signal that the present world will be destroyed and replaced with another, or rather in terms of the transformation and renewal of all that currently exists? Our answer to that question will have far-reaching ethical implications, especially in the field of environmental ethics. Is the earth to be plundered for all it is worth without thought for the future because in the end, it will pass away, or is the earth to be treasured and its goodness preserved because it too will be gathered into God's purposes of transformation and renewal? The former view envisages the earth's annihilation, while the second looks forward to the earth's perfection and renewal and calls for our participation in the conservation and wise habitation of our earthly environment. The annihilationist view seems to be warranted if Revelation 21:1 is taken in isolation or put alongside 2 Peter 3:12–13, but when read alongside Revelation 4 and 5, which portray the whole creation gathered at the end in praise of God, or when read in light of a number of Old Testament passages that envisage the replenishment of the earth and its renewed fruitfulness, the preservation and restoration of creation, rather than its annihilation, emerges as a strong biblical possibility.

The implications for environmental ethics of a vision of salvation that incorporates the whole of creation are being explored across the theological spectrum. Despite adopting quite different approaches to the matter, ecofeminist theologians like Sally McFague and Rosemary Radford Ruether share a deep theological concern for the environment with those who drafted 'An Evangelical Declaration on the Care of Creation'.

Whatever the timing may be of the coming kingdom of God, whether it is present in its fullness already or not yet, and whatever may become of the heavens and the earth through the future realisation of God's purpose, it is important to investigate the substance of these biblical concepts. What is meant by the kingdom of God and what is envisaged in the biblical hope for creation as a whole?

THE KINGDOM OF GOD

It was especially during the nineteenth century that scholars drew attention to the prominence of the kingdom of God in the teaching of Jesus. Whereas the church has often focussed its presentation of the gospel on the forgiveness of sin and the new life made possible through Jesus' death and resurrection, Jesus himself appears to have focussed his teaching on the kingdom of God, with a view to encouraging our participation in that coming reality. But what does the kingdom of God consist in? The words of the Welsh poet and Anglican priest R. S. Thomas (1913–2000) provide a useful indication of the substance of Jesus' teaching about the kingdom. In a poem called 'The Kingdom', Thomas writes:

> It's a long way off but inside it
> There are quite different things going on:
> Festivals at which the poor man
> Is king and the consumptive is
> Healed; mirrors in which the blind look
> At themselves and love looks at them
> Back; and industry is for mending
> The bent bones and the minds fractured
> By life. It's a long way off, but to get
> There takes no time and admission
> Is free, if you will purge yourself
> Of desire, and present yourself with
> Your need only and the simple offering
> Of your faith, green as a leaf.
>
> (R. S. Thomas, *Later Poems*, p. 35)

Thomas' suggestion that in the kingdom of God 'There are quite different things going on' captures a key element of Jesus' proclamation of the kingdom. In the kingdom of God, things are differently ordered. The last shall be first, the poor hear good news, captives are set free and the blind see. These features of Jesus' teaching and of his ministry are signs of God's reordering of things, of God's conforming the world to his good purposes. Healing and justice and reconciliation are hallmarks of this new reality and, as Thomas suggests, 'Industry is for mending … ' That is to say, the gifts of human industry and invention will be directed towards the welfare of all rather than being used in the service of greed and war and selfish ambition. The Bible offers numerous images in support of this expectation that God's ordering of things will one day be complete. A particularly memorable instance is the prophetic vision of a day when the nations 'will beat their swords into ploughshares and their spears into pruning hooks. Nation will not take up sword against nation, nor will they train for war anymore' (Isaiah 2:4; cf. Joel 3:10).

Jesus takes up this prophetic tradition from the Old Testament, tells numerous parables that speak of God's reordering of things and brings about the new reality through his own actions. He eats with tax-collectors and sinners, with those who were despised and who existed on the fringes of society. He heals the sick; he commends the humble and the meek; and he declares that the kingdom of God is for the poor. Jesus turns upside down the way things are typically arranged, or rather, he turns things right side up. In accordance with the theme of reversal, of turning things upside down, a recurring theme of Jesus' parables is that the kingdom is not established as we might expect it to be. It is, Jesus says, like a mustard seed that is the smallest of seeds but grows into a large tree so that birds come and perch in its branches (Matthew 13:31–32). Or it is like yeast mixed into dough (Matthew 13:33). The presence of the kingdom seems at first to be small and insignificant, but its transformative power is far-reaching. The parables of the kingdom reveal too that the kingdom of God is inhabited by the most unlikely people. In Matthew 22:1–10, Jesus says that

> The kingdom of heaven may be compared to a king who gave a wedding banquet for his son. He sent his slaves to call those who had been invited to the wedding banquet, but they would not come. Again he sent other slaves, saying, 'Tell those who have been invited: Look, I have prepared my dinner, my oxen and my fat calves have been slaughtered, and everything is ready; come to the wedding banquet.' But they made light of it and went away, one to his farm, another to his business, while the rest seized his slaves, maltreated them, and killed them. The king was enraged. He sent his troops, destroyed those murderers, and burned their city. Then he said to his slaves, 'The wedding is ready, but those invited were not worthy. Go therefore into the main streets, and

> invite everyone you find to the wedding banquet.' Those slaves went out
> into the streets and gathered all whom they found, both good and bad;
> so the wedding hall was filled with guests.

There are all sorts of interesting allusions in this parable, and in the
further parts of it not quoted here, but the important point for the
present purposes is to notice that those eventually excluded from
the banquet were not excluded for lack of an invitation. Their
interests in maintaining the status quo, through tending the farm and
engaging in business, blinded them to the opportunity they were
being offered to enter into a joyous celebration of the son's wedding,
itself an allusion to the 'marriage' of Christ with his people. So the
net was cast wider and the slaves gathered in all whom they could
find, 'both good and bad'. The kingdom of God is, in principle,
open to all. That some refuse the invitation is not God's intent, but
it remains a possibility. It is not God's way to coerce participation in
his ordering of things. We remain free to refuse, but as the dramatic
burning of the city reveals, the old order to which we often cling
has no future. The Christian hope is that God's ordering of things
will one day be complete, for it is God's order, rather than our
own, that brings life and joy and blessing in the end.

The biblical vision of the kingdom of God has striking political
implications. Jesus' concern for the poor, for the outcast, for the
sick, for children, and his declaration that the kingdom belongs
to such as these (Matthew 19:14; Luke 18:16) entails a new way of
ordering our life together. Although Jesus invites our participation
in this new social order, the kingdom of God cannot be achieved
by conventional political means. It is God himself who will finally
establish his reign throughout all creation. In the meantime, signs of
the coming kingdom appear already in history as hearts and minds
are transformed by the Spirit of God, and as people are drawn by
the Spirit to participate in Christ's life of compassionate service
to others.

A NEW HEAVEN AND A NEW EARTH

The promise given in Revelation 21:1 of a new heaven and a new
earth expresses the biblical expectation that the whole of creation
will be included in the victory over sin and death brought about

through the life, death and resurrection of Christ. Paul expresses this hope in his letter to the church in Rome.

> For the creation waits with eager longing for the revealing of the children of God; for the creation was subjected to futility, not of its own will but by the will of the one who subjected it, in hope that the creation itself will be set free from its bondage to decay and will obtain the freedom of the glory of the children of God.
>
> (Romans 8:19–21)

Paul here echoes the expectation of the Old Testament prophets that salvation is not merely a spiritual matter. It involves the whole of the physical world. A striking feature of Isaiah's vision of the future is that all of God's creatures will live harmoniously together. As he puts it in Isaiah 11:6–7,

> The wolf shall live with the lamb,
> the leopard shall lie down with the kid,
> the calf and the lion and the fatling together,
> and a little child shall lead them.
> The cow and the bear shall graze,
> their young shall lie down together;
> and the lion shall eat straw like the ox.

Elsewhere Isaiah envisages that the deliverance of God's people from exile and bondage will be accompanied by the replenishment of creation (see Isaiah 35:1–2).

The fulfillment of God's purposes for creation has sometimes been portrayed as a return to the garden of Eden, but this is a misrepresentation of the biblical vision that looks towards the world's completion and perfection rather than hoping for a return to its original state. History is not circular in the biblical understanding, but has a linear trajectory towards fulfilment in reconciled communion with God. According to the second-century theologian Irenaeus, the world is not created by God in its final completed state, but, like a newborn baby, it must grow up into maturity and be perfected through union with Christ. According to St Basil, one of the theologians of the early church whom we met earlier, this is the Spirit's work. Basil explains in *The Holy Spirit*, IX; XVI, that the

Spirit is the perfecting cause of creation, the one who brings things to their true and proper end.

What this final order of things will look like and how it will come about we cannot say in detail, but Christian faith confesses that the life, death and resurrection of Jesus provides the decisive clue to the shape of God's future. The resurrection of the body is a crucial element in this future, for the New Testament proclaims that Jesus' resurrection was not merely a spiritual reality. The tomb was left empty and his whole person, body, mind and spirit, was raised from death. This provides the basis of the Christian hope that the whole of created reality, both material and spiritual, will be taken up into the new life that is both inaugurated and foreshadowed through the life, death and resurrection of Jesus.

ETERNAL LIFE

One of the most well-known verses of the Bible is John 3:16: 'For God so loved the world that he gave his only Son, so that everyone who believes in him may not perish but may have eternal life.' The gift of eternal life clearly does not mean that those who believe will not die. It is the fate of all creatures that their lives as we know them will come to an end and they will return to the dust from which they were made (see Genesis 3:19). The biblical promise of eternal life should not be confused with the Greek idea of the immortality of the soul. Greek philosophers like Socrates and Plato envisaged an immortal soul that would continue beyond death, having been freed from the limitations of the body. But this is not the Christian hope. According to the biblical view of creaturely existence, there is no part of us that survives death. The Christian hope for eternal life rests, rather, in God's promise of resurrection.

A second misunderstanding of eternal life is the supposition that those who die will, after the temporary interruption of death, simply be resuscitated and begin a new stretch of temporal existence, this time without end. The Bible, however, seems to envisage something a little different. While the idea that the redeemed will enjoy God's presence *forever* is certainly an expected feature of eternal life, the gathering up and the healing of the whole of history is just as important. The past is not simply lost or left behind. It is redeemed. The brokenness, the pain, the suffering of all creation will be healed and all the tears of history will be wiped from our eyes. Nothing of value will be lost, but all that accords with God's purpose for the creation will be gathered into God's presence, where it will be finally perfected and so take its place in the praise of God's glory.

When speaking of eternal life, the biblical focus usually falls upon the quality of that life rather than its quantity. So, for instance, Jesus in a prayer to the Father says, 'And this is eternal life, that they may know you, the only true God, and Jesus Christ whom you have sent' (John 17:3). Similarly, the eschatological vision in Revelation 21 stresses the presence of God with his people and the transformation in the quality of their lives:

> See, the home of God is among mortals.
> He will dwell with them as their God;
> they will be his peoples,
> and God himself will be with them;
> he will wipe every tear from their eyes.
> Death will be no more;
> mourning and crying and pain will be no more,
> for the first things have passed away.
> And the one who was seated on the throne said,
> 'See, I am making all things new.'

(Revelation 21:3–4)

Particularly among Roman Catholic theologians, the expectation that we will one day see God 'face to face' and behold his glory is referred to as the 'beatific vision'.

It is in anticipation of that fullness of life in the presence of God that Christians join with others in working already towards the overcoming of suffering and pain, and, as a foretaste of the communion promised when God will dwell with his people, Christians gather already in God's presence to pray, to attend to his word, to offer their praise and to intercede for the world. In these ways, humanity has a share already in the eternal life that will be realised fully beyond death.

HEAVEN AND HELL

Using biblical language, the realm in which God's glory is fully revealed, in which there will be no more death or mourning or pain, and from which all sin and evil have been eliminated, is called heaven. Heaven is that realm in which God's good purposes are perfected and fulfilled. While the impression is sometimes given that heaven is a realm wholly distinct from this world and that it exists someplace else, that view owes more to dualistic ideas in which the material and the spiritual are wholly distinct realities. The hope offered in Revelation 21, however, from which we have just quoted, envisions the fullness of God's presence on earth. God will make his home among mortals. Similarly, in the Lord's prayer taught by Jesus to his disciples, the disciples are encouraged to pray to God, 'Your kingdom come, your will be done on earth as it is in heaven.' In the eschatological vision in the book of Revelation, the same theme appears: 'Then the seventh angel blew his trumpet, and there were loud voices in heaven saying, "The kingdom of the world has become the kingdom of our Lord and of his Messiah, and he will reign for ever and ever"' (Revelation 11:15). The Christian hope is that the day will come when the whole earth will be full of God's glory (Psalm 72:19) and God will be all in all (1 Corinthians 15:28).

The biblical vision of heaven is contrasted with a vision of what reality would be like in the complete absence of God. This vision is called hell. It is portrayed as a realm of misery and suffering, of continuing defiance and sin. Hell is often described as a place of fire where there will be weeping and gnashing of teeth (see, for example, Matthew 13:42). During the medieval period, writers and artists often portrayed hell in very graphic terms and the church used images of hell to frighten people into changing their ways, but in recent times, the focus of Christian discussion about hell has tended to move away from such portrayals. It might be argued, in fact, that the realities of life lived in defiance of God have been all too graphically displayed in our own recent history. The death camps and gas chambers of Nazi Germany; the bloodied and disfigured bodies strewn on the ground following massacres in places like Rwanda, and Kosovo, and northern Nigeria; the destruction wrought by terrorists, and by the weapons of war used in retaliation, all give evidence enough of the hellish consequences of human action taken in defiance of God's purpose for human life as it is revealed in the person of Jesus. Such scenes of devastation and destruction are accurately described as a living hell. Tragically, in all these cases, it is not just the guilty who suffer, but the innocent as well.

HOPE IN THE FACE OF SUFFERING AND EVIL

The kinds of evil and suffering that I have just referred to give rise to the question Why? Why is there evil and suffering in a world that is supposed to have been created by a good God who seeks the best for his creatures? That is a question that has been wrestled with by people of faith for thousands of years, while the alleged impossibility of providing any satisfactory answer has been used by many as an argument in favour of atheism.

In the Greek philosophical tradition, we find people wrestling with the problem at least as far back as Epicurus, who lived three centuries before Christ (341–270 BC). In the Hebrew tradition, the struggle of faith and doubt that is prompted by the existence of suffering goes back at least three hundred years earlier, to the books of Job, Isaiah and some of the Psalms. Much more recently, however, the Scottish philosopher David Hume (1711–76) formulated the problem in its most distinct form. Hume asked,

> Is God willing to prevent evil, but not able? Then he is impotent.
> Is he able, but not willing? Then he is malevolent.
> Is he both able and willing? Why then is there evil?

> The attempt to reconcile the reality of suffering and evil with the existence of a loving and all-powerful God is called theodicy.

It is important to note that there are two distinct ways of framing the question about suffering and evil. The first way, encountered in philosophy textbooks and often favoured by proponents of atheism, treats the problem as essentially theoretical. The problem of evil and suffering is posed as a logical puzzle that needs to be solved, by college students, perhaps, in their first-year philosophy courses. Contrast this with the problem of evil and suffering posed from out of the midst of actual suffering. In this case the question is put as an agonised cry against God, and requires not only philosophical consideration but also pastoral response. This is the question of the Psalmist, for example, who pleads, 'My God, my God, why have you forsaken me? Why are you so far from helping me, from the words of my groaning? O my God, I cry by day but you do not answer; and by night but I find no rest' (Psalm 22). In this case the question is framed as a cry for help to a God who does not seem to answer. We come across this plea often enough. What can be said about God, for example, to the parents of a child dying of leukemia? What can be said to the parents who are woken in the night with news that their son or daughter is dead? What can be said about God to those wives and husbands and children who are left father-less or childless or motherless after a missile fired by their enemies has reduced to rubble the streets in which they live? This is the theological and pastorally oriented question about evil and suffering that looks not for the resolution of a logical difficulty but for a more profound theological response about the presence or absence of God in situations like this when darkness descends and one's world seems to be falling apart.

We have no space here to consider in extensive detail the responses typically discussed in the philosophy textbooks. There are, however, four typical responses. The first is the karma theory or the just deserts theory. This is the view that suffering is best understood as a punishment for sins committed. On some accounts it is God who dishes out the punishment, while in others, as in the karma view, there is simply a law of the universe in which people get what they deserve in the end. There is a grain of truth in this otherwise hopelessly inadequate answer. The grain of truth is that sinful or even foolish actions often have consequences that the offender him- or herself is likely to suffer. The link between cigarette smoking and lung cancer, for example, provides an intelligible account of that parti-cular form of suffering, but only a very small proportion of suffering falls into that category. The karma theory fails to account for a vast amount of innocent suffering that clearly exists.

A second view is called the harmony view. This is the idea that the suffering and evil that weigh heavily upon us now will in the total context of history be of greatly diminished significance. We might understand this view by considering the analogy of a beautiful painting. Concentrating on only a small segment of the painting, we might see the colour and content as dark and depressing, but when we stand back and view the work in its entirety, we see the dark and depressing portion as contributing to a beautiful whole. By analogy, when we see the big picture of life itself, it is argued, and appreciate everything in its proper perspective, we will understand that the suffering we currently experience makes for a richness and harmony in life that we do not as yet understand. Nicholas Wolterstorff, a Christian philosopher, provides a powerful response to this line of argument. Following the death of his son in a mountaineering accident, Wolterstorff says:

> But please: Don't say it's really not so bad. Because it is. Death is awful, demonic. If you think your task as comforter is to tell me that really, all things considered, it's not so bad, you do not sit with me in my grief but place yourself off in the distance, away from me. Over there you are of no help. What I need to hear from you is that you recognize how painful it is. I need to hear from you that you are with me in my desperation.
>
> (Wolterstorff, *Lament for a Son*, p. 34)

A third way in which people try to defend God against the presence of evil in the world has been called the soul-making theory. Advocated in recent years by John Hick (1922–2012), the soul-making theory offers the view that suffering may be turned to God's good purposes of bringing human beings to perfection, and that this constitutes a good enough reason for its existence. While people often testify to certain benefits that may be derived from suffering – they may speak, for instance, of how it has made them a better person – the soul-making theory has numerous problems, not the least of which is the disproportionate suffering endured by many. That suffering might be good for you seems to be a desperately inadequate, even obscene, response to offer the victim of rape or genocide, for example. The soul-making theory is famously opposed by the character of Ivan in Fyodor Dostoyevsky's novel *The Brothers Karamazov*. Ivan protests that he doesn't want any part of God's plans for human happiness if the suffering of innocent children is a necessary means of attaining happiness in the end.

John Hick's version of the soul-making theory is a little more moderate than has been suggested above. Hick contends that while God does not ordain each individual event of suffering, he has made this kind of world, nevertheless, because a world in which suffering may be experienced is the best kind of world for perfecting human beings as moral and spiritual agents. One has still to consider, however, whether the sheer scale of suffering can be defended as a means to some good end.

The fourth argument commonly offered in discussions of theodicy is the free-will defence. The free-will defence, most carefully stated in recent times by Alvin Plantinga, suggests that because God seeks a free and loving relation with human beings, we must be created with free will. Evil and suffering are the outcome of this policy, as humanity abuses its freedom and chooses paths that lead to suffering and evil rather than communion and love. Of all the theories considered here, the free-will defence has the most biblical support, although it does not offer a comprehensive account of why suffering and evil exist. The free-will theory has the merit of taking seriously our own responsibility for the causes of a great deal of suffering. It suggests also that we must be involved in working towards the alleviation of suffering. But it cannot account for the full range of suffering that is experienced in this world. It does not account well for what might be called natural disasters or for a great deal of illness that seems to have no direct relation to human sin. Plantinga himself readily acknowledges this. His purpose in developing the free-will argument is simply to show that the existence of evil and suffering is not logically incompatible with the existence of a loving and all-powerful God. The pastoral questions referred to above, however, have still to be addressed.

These intellectual responses to the problem of suffering and evil give evidence of humanity's wrestling with the problem, but it must be admitted that none are entirely satisfactory. Suffering and evil remain, to some extent, incomprehensible. We have a good understanding of why suffering exists in some circumstances but not in all. Does this make belief in a good and loving God impossible? Many atheists say so, but that conclusion should not be drawn without considering all the other reasons that may be offered for believing in God. The problem of evil and suffering is a troubling one, but it is not intellectually irresponsible to say that while I do not understand why it is that suffering and evil exist on such a scale, there are many other things that persuade me of the existence of God.

Christian theologians have commonly acknowledged that while the intellectual problem remains, the problem of suffering more commonly encountered is the urgent pastoral questions to which suffering gives rise. Where is God to be found, in the face of suffering? How long must this pain be endured? Why does God not come to our aid? The most powerful answers given to these questions in recent times have come from those who have themselves endured great suffering. In the concentration camps of Nazi Germany, in the slums of Latin America and of Asia, and in many other places of deep anguish and suffering, voices have emerged that testify to the presence of God in the midst of terrible human suffering and degradation. One finds testimony to this presence of God in the theology of liberation theologians, for example, working in slums with the poor and the oppressed. One finds it in the testimony of those who have been tortured and persecuted for their faith, for their political views or for the colour of their skin.

One such testimony can be found in the work of Brazilian artist Guido Rocha. Unjustly accused of being a member of a subversive group, imprisoned and tortured, Guido Rocha sees Christ as the brother who has himself known the suffering that the poor of Latin America now endure. When crying out in pain in prison, Rocha remembered the cry of Christ on the cross, 'My God, my God, why have you forsaken me?' This cry of Christ from the cross became for Rocha a great promise. He began to model many images of the tortured Christ, their faces often resembling those of Rocha's fellow prisoners as they cried out under torture. For Rocha, the crucified Christ was an image of hope, that even in the hell of a Brazilian torture chamber God is present. There is no place where God leaves us without his presence. Even in the deepest abyss of human suffering, God is there, taking the burden of it upon himself. To the question of how God relates to human evil and suffering, Christian theology tells the story of one who took upon himself the suffering of the world, who identifies himself with the victims of suffering. In the suffering of Christ, it is revealed that there are no limits to the compassion of God; there is no place that the love of God cannot reach.

Christian theology has no definitive answer to why it is that suffering and evil exist. But it offers testimony to the God who does not remain remote from suffering, who enters into its midst, who sides with those who suffer even to the point of death. The resurrection of Christ from the dead is the promise that suffering and evil have no future. They will in the end be overcome. That hope provides the motivation to protest against suffering and evil wherever its cause can be attributed to human action, and to work in solidarity with all those who struggle against it.

THE LAST JUDGEMENT AND UNIVERSAL SALVATION

A crucial feature of the Christian hope that evil will be overcome is the concept of the last judgement. Because God's purpose is to perfect the creation and to draw all things into reconciled relationship with himself and with one another, evil cannot survive. New Testament scholar and theologian Richard Bauckham (1946–) writes: 'When the truth of all history is finally laid bare before the judgement of God, evil, as evil, must perish. This is not a contradiction to but is required by God's loving and salvific will for all creatures. They must be delivered from evil' (Bauckham, 'Eschatology', p. 319). Judgement involves, above all, a laying bare of the truth of things. It is only God who can do this, for only God sees fully the true nature of things. It is for this reason that Jesus advises against the temptation, frequently indulged, to pass judgement on one another. The parable of the wheat and the tares in Matthew 13:24–30 suggests that we (the servants in the parable) are not very good at judging what or who is good and who is evil. The point of Jesus' parable is that we should leave that judgement to God. There may be a need for interim judgments, such as those pronounced against the evil of criminal offences, for example, or against corruption and injustice, but Jesus' parable cautions against taking the final judgement into our own hands.

Just because God alone is the final judge, we human beings should avoid speculation about what the outcome of God's final judgement will be. The outcome of God's intervention as judge in the person of Jesus Christ surprised religious people most of all. The guardians of the law and of Israel's religious purity were outraged at the judgements Jesus made about those whom the religious authorities were ready to condemn. The story in John 8:1–11, of the woman 'caught in adultery', is one of many suggestions in the gospels that God is more interested in showing mercy and forgiveness than in condemning those who fail. The story provides further inducement to let God do the judging. The responsibility of Christians is to follow where Christ leads rather than to take the prerogative of judgment upon themselves.

The mercy and forgiveness shown by Jesus to sinners raises the question of whether all might be saved in the end. The Bible does not settle that question. There are certainly verses that warn against the dire consequences of human sin and of the refusal to trust in God (e.g. Matthew 25:46), but there are also verses that speak of God's desire that all should be saved (e.g. 1 Timothy 2:4). The apostle Paul wrestles with this matter in Romans 10–11. Paul is concerned that his own people Israel have not recognised Jesus as saviour and Lord, but he insists that God has not abandoned Israel. He proclaims that 'all Israel will be saved' (Romans 11:26). While Paul has explained earlier that all who confess with their lips that Jesus is Lord and believe in their heart that God raised him from the dead will be saved (Romans 10:9), he has not given up on those who have not confessed and who have not yet believed. He trusts that in the end God will work things out and will bring his covenant with Israel to fulfilment. That seems to be the appropriate attitude for Christians to hold in relation to others who do not share their belief. While leaving the final outcome to God, it would seem appropriate too for Christians in the meantime to follow Paul in devoting their lives to the proclamation of the good news.

OTHER RELIGIONS

Towards the end of the twentieth century, a number of theologians became interested in the 'problem' of religious plurality. Christianity is not the only religious game in town. And yet the Christian church has commonly claimed that salvation comes through Christ alone. What is to be made of the fact that there are many other religious paths on offer? Despite claims to the contrary by John Hick, Paul Knitter and others who have become advocates of religious pluralism, this is not a problem that Christians have become aware of only in recent times. The fact that there are many religions offering competing claims about the nature of God, and about the nature of our human situation, is nothing new. That reality has been known and repeatedly addressed throughout the Bible and throughout Christian history. What is new is the suggestion that Christians should respond to this plurality of religious options by accepting that all religious faiths are legitimate paths to the one God who is addressed and is understood in different ways by the various religions. That view is known as religious pluralism, and the implication of it is that Christians should abandon their exclusive claim that Jesus is the only way to salvation.

In his promotion of religious pluralism, John Hick commends a saying from a Hindu text, the Bhagavad Gita, which reads as follows: 'Howsoever men may approach me, even so do I accept them; for on all sides, whatever path men choose is mine.' The text suggests that in the matter of religious faith, every path is as valid as any other, and Krishna or God or the ultimate being in the universe will accept every path as leading to the divine. At face value, this appears to be an attractive philosophy. It promotes the virtues of tolerance of others and goodwill to all. Despite these apparent virtues, however, the position advocated by the Bhagavad Gita does not survive close scrutiny. Whatever path people choose is mine, it says, supposedly in the name of God, but human beings have chosen paths in the name of God that have led to child sacrifice and burning witches at the stake. They have chosen paths in the name of God that have led to inquisitions and crusades and the brutal slaying of those who do not agree with their religious convictions. In the name of God, human beings have chosen to slice off the hands of those who break their religious laws or to execute those who are thought to have blasphemed against their God. In the name of God, men and women carry arms and plant bombs that kill children and tear communities to shreds. Are we really to suppose that all paths followed in the name of religious conviction have equal value and lead to God in the end? A simple ethical judgement about the paths human beings do sometimes choose makes that claim implausible.

One of the reasons why people make the claim that all religions are basically on the right track is because they are concerned for the salvation of all people. If God is a God of love, then surely he cannot condemn those millions of people who, through no fault of their own, have never heard of Jesus Christ and who have lived devout lives in obedience to the demands of some other religious tradition. It seems arrogant to suggest that such people cannot be saved, and it calls into question whether God is really a God of justice and of love.

The writings of John Hick again provide an instance of this view. Hick argues that there is abundant evidence in all religions of people who live good and upright and impressively compassionate lives yet do not confess any faith in Jesus Christ. It is morally out-rageous to suggest that God is going to condemn them just because they have never had the opportunity to hear the good news that Christianity proclaims. This argument deserves serious considera-tion. Because one's religious faith seems to depend, to some extent at least, on an accident of birth, where is the justice in suggesting that only those born into a Christian environment have any real chance at salvation? The child born in India who becomes a Hindu, or the child born in Thailand who becomes a Buddhist, can hardly be blamed for not believing in Jesus Christ. Must Christianity not concede that the genuine devotion and good works of people of other faiths will be approved by God and will lead to their salvation, regardless of Jesus Christ?

There is no denying the impressive devotion and the compas-sionate service often rendered by people of other faiths, or of none. But it is also worth noting that this view of the merits of other religious practices and beliefs turns salvation into something that we earn. It is salvation by works. Christianly conceived, that is not very good news. It places a burden upon us to meet certain moral standards, to fulfil certain devotional requirements, and to attain merit for ourselves through good works. It has been shown many times that this view of how salvation may be attained is open to exploitation by unscrupulous religious leaders who demand more and more by way of devotion and service and monetary offerings in order that their followers may attain salvation. To be sure, all of these things – an upright life, religious devotion and works of service and compas-sion – are good things, and each has its place in the Christian life, but, Christianly conceived again, these things are not the *conditions* of salvation. They are not requirements to be met before God will show favour to us. Rather they are the practices that flow in joyous response from the news that while we were yet sinners, Christ died for us (Romans 5:8). The idea that salvation depends on our good works is, according to Karl Barth, a form of unbelief. It amounts to a denial of the claim made in 2 Corinthians 5:19 that God was in Christ reconciling the world to himself. The Christian good news is that God, in Christ, has done what is necessary for the world's salvation. God has done, in fact, what we cannot do for ourselves. According to Paul, God has done this for 'the world'.

The confession of the uniqueness of Christ can in this way be seen as a radically inclusive claim. Christ has died for every member of the human family, irrespective of their piety, of their upbringing, of their spiritual sensitivity or religious devotion, and irrespective of their ethical accomplishment. Paul goes on in 2 Corinthians 5 to describe Christians as those to whom this message of reconciliation has been entrusted. Christians have a task to perform, therefore, as bearers of this message in the context of dialogue with people of other faiths. The content of the message itself, however, means that Christians must give up any sense of superiority in their dealings with people of other religions. The truth to which Christianity bears witness is a truth that humbles and yet that also gives hope for the whole of humankind.

The gospel of grace that I have been referring to gives rise among some theologians to the concern that it removes the incentive for evangelism. If the message that God will punish in hellfire those who do not believe is robbed of its power, then where is the incentive to proclaim the gospel? The incentive lies in the content of the good news itself. In his article on world mission, 'All Things New', Alan Lewis puts it well: sinners should know of their forgiveness. The captives should know of their release. Those who walk in darkness should know that the light has come. This is the news that Christians have to share in respectful dialogue with people of other faiths.

THE RETURN OF CHRIST

We have noted already the emphasis in the Bible upon all things being completed or fulfilled 'on the last day'. In the New Testament, that completion and fulfillment is bound up with the completion of the work of Christ. Following his account in 1 Corinthians 15 of the expected resurrection of the dead, the apostle Paul says, 'Then comes the end, when [Christ] hands over the kingdom to God the Father, after he has destroyed every ruler and every authority and power' (1 Corinthians 15:24). In order to hand the kingdom over to the Father, Christ is elsewhere envisaged as coming again to gather all things to himself. This expectation of Christ's return is a core belief of Christian faith, expressed as follows in the Nicene Creed: 'He will come again in glory to judge the living and the dead, and his kingdom will have no end.' Unfortunately, the promise of Christ's return has often given rise to highly speculative accounts of when and where and in what way Christ will return, but Jesus himself is portrayed in Matthew's gospel as offering a caution against such speculation: 'But about that day and hour no one knows, neither the angels of heaven, nor the Son, but only the Father' (Matthew 24:36).

The Greek word 'parousia', meaning presence or arrival, is commonly used by theologians to refer to the return of Christ.

Wild speculation about when and how Christ will return is best avoided, but the emphasis placed upon the return of Christ in the New Testament should inspire confidence among Christians that the world's future rests in God's hands and that all creation will be brought under the Lordship of Christ. His return in glory will complete the work of redemption in which sin and death will finally be overcome and all things will be reconciled to the Father.

THE GLORY OF GOD

If we were to ask, what is the central and overriding theme of Christian theology, theologians would no doubt offer a range of answers. A compelling case could be made, however, that Christian theology is concerned, above all, to bear witness to the glory of God. It is for the sake of God's glory that creation is brought into being, and through creation the glory of God is revealed (Psalm 19:1). Israel too is created for God's glory (Isaiah 43:7) and is appointed to be a witness among the nations to the glory of God (Isaiah 49:3).

The writers of the New Testament testify that the glory of God is revealed most especially in Jesus Christ (Hebrews 1:3; John 1:14), while John's gospel repeatedly suggests that the work of Christ, reaching its climax in his death and resurrection, is the means by which God is glorified (John 12:27–28). Human beings are to participate in this glory (2 Corinthians 3:18) and are called to live 'for the praise of God's glory' (Ephesians 1:12). The Westminster Catechism of the Reformed tradition expresses this point by affirming that the chief end of human beings is to glorify God and to enjoy him forever. The revelation of God's glory is, finally, a strong feature of the biblical hope. Speaking to the people of Israel during times of hardship and suffering, the prophet Isaiah looks forward to the day when 'the glory of the Lord shall be revealed, and all people shall see it together' (Isaiah 40:5). That hope is expressed again in Isaiah 60:19–21 and is echoed in Revelation 21:23, in which a future heavenly city is envisaged in which there will be no sun and no moon, for the glory of the Lord will be its light.

All this talk in the Bible of God's desire that he should be glorified might give rise to the impression that God is engaged in some kind of ego trip, as though he were an insecure monarch needing to be flattered by the praises of his subjects. Such an impression, however, could arise only if we divorced the biblical talk of God's glory from the story of divine compassion and love that is told in the Bible. God is majestic and his glory is resplendent, to be sure, but the resplendence of God's glory and the majesty of God are revealed above all in Christ, and especially through his suffering. The glory of God is revealed as the Son of God meets with tax-collectors and sinners, seeks out the lost and the heavy-laden, heals the sick, offers good news to the poor and makes his way to Calvary, where he takes upon himself the world's suffering and sin. The Son does this so that a world that goes its way in defiance of God may be gathered again into the realm of God's glory and love. To suggest, therefore, that God seeks praise of his glory is simply to say that God desires that all creation should live within the embrace of his love, that all should live in the light of his glory rather than in the darkness. God's desire that his glory should fill the earth is the expression of his care for all creation.

The fulfilment of that goal rests in what God has done in Christ and continues to do through the work of the Spirit. Through the

work of the Son and the Spirit, creation is drawn to participate in
the life-giving communion of God's love. Thus Jesus prays, 'As
you, Father, are in me and I am in you, may they also be in us so that
the world may believe that you have sent me' (John 17:21). The glory
of God expresses itself, not in self-glorifying majesty, but in the
extravagant communication of God's own fullness of life. Frequently
in the Bible the metaphor of the wedding feast is employed to speak
of this joyous relationship into which God draws his people. In
John's gospel, for example, the first sign of the abundance of life
that Jesus will bring is the turning of water into wine that takes
place at a wedding feast in Cana. John comments that in doing this
Jesus revealed his glory (see John 2:1–11). In Matthew's gospel the
parable of the wedding feast serves as a witness to the abundant
blessing that God wishes to shower upon his people. The people
who keep company with Jesus are described as wedding guests
(Mark 2:19; Matthew 9:15; Luke 5:34) because they are people
who have begun to share in the loving communion and in the
glory of God. The final fulfilment of God's purposes is imagined in
Revelation 19:7 as the 'marriage of the lamb'. Even the heavenly
Jerusalem comes down from heaven to human beings 'like a bride
adorned for her husband' (Revelation 21:2), and the final vision of
Revelation is of the joining of the Spirit and the Bride.

> The Spirit and the Bride say, 'Come'.
> And let everyone who hears say, 'Come'.
> And let everyone who is thirsty come,
> Let everyone who wishes take the water of life as gift.
>
> (Revelation 21:17)

The most prevalent characteristic of wedding feasts is joy. So in
John's gospel, Jesus' joy will remain in those who are his, so that
their 'joy may be full' (John 15:11). This is what is sought for all
creation in the biblical hope that God's glory will be revealed.

A story is told of the great Russian composer, doctor and scientist
Alexander Borodin that one day he sat at the piano with his young
daughter, who was making her own not very beautiful sounds on
the piano. Borodin placed his own hands on the keys outside hers
and wove her tuneless notes into a beautiful piece of music. This is
what it means for the glory of God to be revealed. God does not

need us to show forth his glory. Nor does he need the praise that is creation's proper response to his glory. In a similar way, Borodin did not need his daughter in order to make glorious music, but the inclusion of her notes showed forth his glory all the more. It was a glory revealed in the tender love that a father had for his daughter and in his desire that her playing, stumbling and tuneless though it was, should be woven into a reality that was full of beauty and joy. So it is with God's relationship with his 'children'. This is what it means for the glory of God to be revealed.

A central element of Christian faith is the hope that one day God's purposes will be brought to fulfilment, that his glory will fill the earth, and that all flesh shall see it together. In the meantime, Christians are called to give expression to that hope through worship, through intercession for the world, through proclamation and through lives of compassionate service to others. That calling will be the subject of our next and final chapter.

FOR FURTHER READING

General treatments of the theme of eschatology are offered by Richard Bauckham, 'Eschatology', in *The Oxford Handbook of Systematic Theology*, edited by John Webster, Kathryn Tanner and Iain Torrance (Oxford: Oxford University Press, 2007), 306–22, and Daniel Migliore, *Faith Seeking Understanding* (Grand Rapids, MI: Eerdmans, 1991), ch.12. A more extensive treatment can be found in Jürgen Moltmann, *The Coming of God: Christian Eschatology* (London: SCM Press, 1996). The cosmic scope of the work of Christ is helpfully considered in Teresa Okure, SHJC, 'The Global Jesus', in Markus Bockmuehl, ed., *The Cambridge Companion to Jesus* (Cambridge: Cambridge University Press, 2001), 237–49. The ways in which the kingdom of God turns upside down our customary ways of ordering the world are explored by Stanley Hauerwas in *The Peaceable Kingdom: A Primer in Christian Ethics* (London: SCM Press, 1983).

The problem of evil is helpfully addressed in Kenneth Surin, *Theology and the Problem of Evil* (Oxford: Blackwell, 1986), while in *The Crucified God* (London: SCM Press, 1974), Jürgen Moltmann provides a powerful exposition of God's identification with the victims of evil and suffering.

The Myth of Christian Uniqueness (London: SCM Press, 1988), edited by Paul F. Knitter, gathers together a number of essays by advocates of religious pluralism, while contrary views may be found in Lesslie Newbigin, *The Gospel in a Pluralist Society* (Grand Rapids, MI: Eerdmans, 1989), and Gavin D'Costa, 'The Impossibility of a Pluralist View of Religions', in *Religious Studies* 32.2 (June 1996), 223–32.

The 'Evangelical Declaration on the Care of Creation' can be found in R. J. Berry, ed., *The Care of Creation: Focussing Concern and Action* (Leicester: Inter-Varsity Press, 2000). Other useful treatments of this theme are collected in *Environmental Stewardship: Critical Perspectives Past and Present,* ed. R. J. Berry (London: T&T Clark, 2006).

A NEW COMMUNITY

The news that God has raised Jesus from the dead is earth-shattering news. It is news that calls into question our prior understandings of what kind of world it is that we live in. It is news that reveals a divine limitation on humanity's capacity to destroy what God has made. It reveals, for those who have eyes to see, that God is at work in the world bringing to completion his purposes. If all of this is true, then the question inevitably arises, what next? If Jesus has been raised from the dead, what now is our human reality? And what now is to be done?

The four gospels respond to this last question with an instruction that is brief and to the point. In Matthew's gospel, we read that the risen Christ appears to the disciples and says,

> All authority in heaven and earth has been given to me. Go therefore and make disciples of all nations, baptizing them in the name of the Father and of the Son and of the Holy Spirit, and teaching them to obey everything that I have commanded you. And remember, I am with you always, to the end of the age.
>
> (Matthew 28:19–20)

In Luke's gospel, Jesus meets with the disciples, explains to them that all that has happened through his life, his death and his resurrection is the fulfilment of Scripture's story, the story of God's dealings with Israel and of God's promise that all the families of the earth will be blessed.

> Thus it is written, [Jesus says] that the Messiah is to suffer and to rise from the dead on the third day, and that repentance and forgiveness of sins is to be proclaimed in his name to all nations, beginning from Jerusalem. You are witnesses of these things. And see, I am sending upon you what my Father promised; so stay here in the city until you have been clothed with power from on high.
>
> (Luke 24:45–49)

The conclusion to John's gospel is rather more enigmatic, but the high point of John's final chapter is undoubtedly the instruction given to the disciple Peter. Following Peter's threefold denial of Jesus at the time of Jesus' arrest and crucifixion (see John 18:17, 25–27), Jesus now asks Peter three times whether Peter loves him, and, in response to Peter's remorseful confession of allegiance, Jesus commissions him to tend and to feed 'my sheep'. There are echoes here of a conversation recorded earlier in the gospel in which Jesus speaks of himself as the good shepherd who lays down his life for those he loves (see John 10:1–18). Peter is called to take up the responsibility of caring for those whom Jesus loves.

The ending of Mark's gospel is somewhat problematic. The most authentic version we have among the ancient manuscripts ends very abruptly. It appears that a final page may have been lost. In other manuscripts, two different endings have been added, in order, apparently, to replace the lost ending. Both suggested endings involve Jesus' commissioning of the disciples to 'go into all the world and proclaim the good news to the whole creation' (Mark 14:15).

In answer to the question 'What is to be done in the light of Jesus' resurrection from the dead?' the gospel writers make clear that this news is to be proclaimed. The new reality is to be made known to all nations; people are to be invited to participate in the new life that Christ has established, and they are to be fed and tended like a long-lost prodigal son who returns to the embrace of his father's love. The gospels conclude with a commission. Because Jesus has been raised, because sin and death have been overcome once and for all, the news should be declared to the nations that

God has responded to our defiance with forgiveness, and to our rebellion with the promise of new life.

ASCENSION AND PENTECOST

The way that this task of proclamation was taken up by the first disciples of Jesus is described in the Acts of the Apostles, a continuation by the same author of the story told in the gospel of Luke. The book of Acts begins with the story of one last encounter with the risen Christ before telling of Jesus' ascension 'to heaven'. We are not to imagine here, I suggest, a journey through space as if Jesus had left the earth like an astronaut headed for the 'heavens'. The key point to understand, rather, is that the risen Christ is now present with the Father where, along with the Spirit, he continues the work of drawing the world into communion with God. At various points in the New Testament, both Christ and the Spirit are presented as interceding for the world. They represent the world's need before the Father, its need for forgiveness and healing and new life. Speaking metaphorically, the Son and the Spirit are the arms of God extended towards the world and gathering it into God's presence. The Son himself, truly God and truly human, as the ancient creeds have it, is present with the Father with the wounds of crucifixion still present in his human body, and so takes to the Father's heart the suffering of humankind. It is at the Father's side that the Son intercedes for the world, and holds it in love, until that day when Jesus will hand over the kingdom to the Father and all things will be made complete.

Before ascending to the Father, Jesus reiterates a promise that has been heard several times before, both in his own teaching and in the Old Testament: 'the Holy Spirit will come upon you'. There is a very important sense in which the Spirit of God is always present in creation, giving breath to all that lives and sustaining the life that is God's gift to the world. But the Bible speaks also of a pouring out of the Spirit in ways that bring about radical transformation. The Spirit lifts the world beyond mere existence into the realm of abundant life that is God's purpose for it. The transformations brought about through the Spirit's presence are sometimes dramatic, such as were seen on the day of Pentecost reported in Acts 2. The believers 'were all together in one place', we are told.

> And suddenly from heaven there came a sound like the rush of a violent wind, and it filled the entire house where they were sitting. Divided tongues, as of fire, appeared among them, and a tongue rested on each of them. All of them were filled with the Holy Spirit and began to speak in other languages, as the Spirit gave them ability.
>
> (Acts 2:2–4)

The presence of God's Spirit is not always accompanied by such dramatic events; sometimes the presence of God is known through a still, small voice (1 Kings 19:11–13), and is apparent in quiet acts of compassion and forgiveness, but there are also times when God's presence is revealed through phenomena such as speaking in tongues, dramatic healings and the conversion of great numbers of people. We have seen this in our own time through the emergence of the Charismatic and Pentecostal movements and through the rapid spread of Christianity through Asia, Africa and Latin America. The outpouring of the Holy Spirit through these movements and in these places is often accompanied by dramatic works of the Spirit like those spoken of in the New Testament, and is a means by which God brings about the revival of his people and the spread of the gospel. Whether in quiet and unassuming ways or through the much more dramatic transformation of people's lives, the work of the Spirit gives a foretaste of God's coming kingdom that was inaugurated and foreshadowed in the resurrection of Jesus from the dead. A repeated assertion of the biblical story is that the Spirit gives life (John 6:63; 2 Corinthians 3:6). Put another way, the gift of the Spirit is the means by which God enlivens and equips his people and makes them a witness to his transformative work in the world.

In the account given in Acts 2 of the outpouring of the Spirit among the first Christian believers, we are told that those present did not know what to make of it. 'All were amazed and perplexed, saying to one another, "What does this mean?"' (Acts 2:12). The disciple Peter, who had been entrusted, as we have seen, with the task of tending Christ's sheep, addressed the crowd and gave an explanation of what was going on. He began by reminding them of the promise found in the Old Testament:

> In the last days it will be, God declares,
> that I will pour out my Spirit upon all flesh,

> and your sons and your daughters shall prophesy,
> and your young men shall see visions,
> and your old men shall dream dreams.
> Even upon my slaves, both men and women,
> in those days I will pour out my Spirit;
> and they shall prophesy ...
>
> (Acts 2:17–18; cf. Joel 2:28–29)

Peter then goes on to explain that this outpouring of the Spirit is prompted by the raising of Jesus from the dead. 'This Jesus God raised up ... Being therefore exalted at the right hand of God and having received from the Father the promise of the Holy Spirit, he has poured out this that you see and hear' (Acts 2:33). Peter declares that the promise given to Israel is now being fulfilled through Christ and through the Spirit. God is extending his blessing to all nations. That is, in part, the significance of those who were present hearing the gospel proclaimed in their own languages. The promise of blessing is no longer restricted to Israel. In fact, it never was. God desires that all people should be drawn into the embrace of his love (1 Timothy 2:4). When those who were watching the scene heard Peter's explanation of what was going on, they said to him, 'What should we do?' and Peter replied, 'Repent and be baptised everyone of you in the name of Jesus Christ so that your sins may be forgiven; and you will receive the gift of the Holy Spirit. For the promise is for you, for your children, and for all who are far away, everyone whom the Lord our God calls to him' (Acts 2:37–38).

THE BEGINNING OF THE CHURCH

There are a number of moments in the biblical story that could be described as the beginning of the Christian church – the calling of the disciples, their commissioning after the resurrection of Jesus, or even, as some suggest, the calling of Abraham and Sarah. While it isn't particularly important to be able to identify a single moment when the church began, the day of Pentecost is regarded by many as the day on which the church was founded. Certainly, there are a number of elements in the story of Pentecost that remain central to the nature of the church in its many variant forms throughout

Christian history and across the globe. These include the gift of the Spirit, the preaching of the good news of Jesus in continuity with Israel's story, baptism, the breaking of bread, prayer, fellowship, devotion to the apostles' teaching, the sharing of a common life and worship. All of these are mentioned in Acts 2 and are features that one would expect to see in any community that calls itself a Christian church.

THE GIFT OF THE SPIRIT

We have seen in earlier chapters that the Spirit of God is present throughout creation, giving and sustaining life. But we have seen also God's promise of a special work of the Spirit that draws people into communion with God and equips them to be the bearers of his word and participants with Christ in God's coming kingdom. The Spirit of God poured out at Pentecost is a Spirit who converts hearts and minds to a knowledge of and faith in Christ. The Spirit then equips those who have responded to God's call upon them to be his witnesses throughout the world. They are equipped for mission and for service. Writing to the church in Corinth, the apostle Paul describes various gifts of the Spirit that are given to the church.

> Now there are varieties of gifts, but the same Spirit; and there are varieties of services, but the same Lord; and there are varieties of activities, but it is the same God who activates all of them in everyone. To each is given the manifestation of the Spirit for the common good. To one is given through the Spirit the utterance of wisdom, and to another the utterance of knowledge according to the same Spirit, to another faith by the same Spirit, to another gifts of healing by the one Spirit, to another the working of miracles, to another prophecy, to another the discernment of spirits, to another various kinds of tongues, to another the interpretation of tongues. All these are activated by one and the same Spirit, who allots to each one individually just as the Spirit chooses.

> (1 Corinthians 12:4–11)

This is not an exhaustive list of gifts given by the Spirit to enable our participation in the work God is doing in the world. There are many other gifts given by the Spirit that are to be used in building up the church, in service of others and in proclaiming the gospel throughout the world. Indeed, Paul makes the point in the surrounding verses of this passage that all members of the Body of Christ are given gifts that are to be valued equally and used together in the life of the Christian community. The Holy Spirit is sometimes spoken of as if 'it' were simply a form of divine power or energy, but this should be avoided. The Spirit, along with the Father and the Son, is one of the three persons of the Trinity, so whenever the Spirit is spoken of, we are speaking of God's presence in person. Wherever the gifts of the Spirit are evident, therefore, God is present, working in and through the people he has called and commissioned to be his people.

> 'The Body of Christ' is one of many images used in the New Testament to describe the church. It is an image that emphasises both the church's participation in the life and work of Christ, and its unity as one body.

THE PREACHING OF THE GOOD NEWS

Peter's proclamation of Christ's death and resurrection, of the coming of the Spirit, and of the way these events should be understood in continuity with all that God has done throughout Israel's history, were a central feature of what took place on the day of Pentecost. It was in response to Peter's message that people's hearts and minds were changed, that they were baptised and that they received the gift of the Spirit. Although people may come to Christian faith through many different paths, somewhere in their experience they must hear the proclamation of the gospel. They must hear the news addressed to them that God has come among us in the person of Christ, who has taken our suffering and our sin upon himself, has died for us, has been raised from the dead and has reconciled the world to God. The church is the community entrusted with that news, that is called to live by it and that is commissioned to proclaim it. Apart from its hearing, its living and its proclamation of this gospel, the church cannot truly be the church. During the Protestant Reformation of the sixteenth century, in a time of dispute about what constituted the true church, the

Reformers argued that the faithful preaching of the word, alongside the 'right administration of the sacraments', is an essential and defining mark of the true church. The proclamation of the gospel is a fundamental characteristic of the church's life.

BAPTISM

It has been argued above that the resurrection of Jesus from the dead is the inauguration of a new reality, of a changed situation in the world whereby sin and death have been robbed of their power to determine the world's future. The resurrection is also the means by which the purpose of God to give abundant life to the creature has been firmly set on its trajectory towards fulfilment. Baptism marks the incorporation of individuals into that new reality. Incorporation into the new reality of life in Christ involves, necessarily, a turning away from the old reality in which sin and death held sway. This turning away is called repentance, and it is symbolised in baptism through immersion in water. Water cleanses but, as Colin Gunton reminds us, it is also the stuff that drowns (Gunton, *The Christian Faith*, p. 145). Both feature in the act of baptism, in which the person baptised is incorporated into the death and resurrection of Christ and so is cleansed of sin and 'made right' with God. In baptism, the person dies to the old life of sin and death and emerges from the water into a new life in communion with Christ and with the people whom Christ calls to be his body, the church. Baptism is an act with a subjective and an objective dimension. It is an act in which the church, along with the individual who is baptised, recognises, accepts and celebrates the objective reality of what God has done and continues to do. Christ has died for us, 'while we were yet sinners', as Paul puts it in Romans 5:8, thus showing forth the love of God that does not wait upon our response but is given unconditionally and without restraint. This forgiving, and reconciling, and unmerited love of God is, as Paul again puts it, a free gift of grace (Ephesians 2:8). And yet it does call for a response. This is the subjective dimension of baptism signified in the promises made in baptism by the person being baptised *or* by the person's parents, and by the particular church community in which the baptism takes place.

The word 'or' in the previous sentence is indicative of a long-standing disagreement in the church about who can be baptised.

Within some traditions it has been the practice to baptise children and infants in order to make clear that all that God has done in Christ has been done for them too, whether or not they understand it. On the other hand, some branches of the church have insisted that baptism requires that the person being baptised personally acknowledges what God has done, repents and commits him- or herself to the life of Christian faith. Both positions have good arguments in their favour. Those who consider infant baptism to be appropriate explain that what God has done for our salvation has been done for all people, regardless of their understanding, or even their acceptance of it. Infant baptism makes it very clear that the baptised person is the recipient of divine grace without having done anything to deserve or to earn it. Furthermore, where a child is raised in the context of the church community, it makes little sense to suggest that they are not part of the new community established in Christ and a beneficiary of all that Christ has done. On the other hand, those who reserve baptism for those who can offer their willing and repentant consent may argue, justifiably, that baptism involves a change, not only of status before God, but also of the life one lives. That change requires the consent and the active commitment of the person concerned. While disagreement on this issue gave rise in the seventeenth century to division in the church, and a separation of those who insisted on believers' baptism from those who practiced infant baptism, and while distinct branches of the church continue to be divided on this issue, difference of opinion on this matter is not often seen today as a barrier to genuine Christian fellowship among people who believe differently.

THE LORD'S SUPPER

The celebration of the Lord's Supper is called by other names across various branches of the Christian church, including the Eucharist, the Mass and Holy Communion.

Twice in the concluding verses of Acts 2, we are told that the breaking of bread was a regular feature of the life of those who believed the gospel and who repented and were baptised. This seems an odd thing to mention except, of course, that the breaking of bread recalls the supper that Jesus shared with his disciples on the night before he was crucified. It is probable that the meal Jesus shared was a Passover meal, a meal celebrated annually by Jews and through which they recall God's deliverance of Israel from slavery in Egypt. The various elements of the Passover meal, unleavened bread, a lamb, green and bitter herbs, fruit puree and wine, recall aspects of the slavery in Egypt and the night when God set Israel free (see Exodus 12). The Passover meal is always accompanied by a liturgy in which the story of Israel's deliverance is taught to the children in every Jewish household. The telling of this story at the Passover meal recalls and confirms for Jewish people that their identity as a people is determined by God's action. They are a people called and appointed by God to be the bearers of his promise. They are a people called to live in covenant relationship with God. They are a people whom God has delivered from bondage.

All of these things would have been running through the minds of the disciples when they shared in the Passover meal with Jesus. Only, when Jesus took bread and broke it and shared it with his disciples, he introduced a new act in the drama. After taking the bread and giving thanks, as was customary, Jesus broke it and said, 'This is my body, which is given for you. Do this in remembrance of me' (Luke 22:19). Then he took the cup of wine, saying, 'This cup that is poured out for you is the new covenant in my blood.'

In setting his own work of salvation, and his imminent death, within the context of the Passover meal, Jesus places himself in this same tradition of divine deliverance and liberation. Just as the Passover story is central to the identity of the Jewish people, so too the Lord's Supper and the story told by means of it are the key to the identity of Christians. Who is a Jew? we might ask. A Jew is likely to reply that a Jew is one whom God has delivered from bondage in Egypt and to whom salvation is given. Who then is a Christian? A Christian is one whom God has delivered from the bondage of sin and death and who has entered into the fellowship of Christ's body. When Christians celebrate the Lord's Supper, they are telling the story of who they are, a people who share in the new covenant, or the new relationship with God, that is established by Christ. The regular 'breaking of bread' in the early church is likely to have been a means, like the Passover meal is for Jews, of telling and teaching the story of the salvation that God has accomplished and of the new identity that is established through God's saving work.

As with baptism, the Lord's Supper has also been a matter about which various Christian churches have disagreed. The principal point of disagreement, hotly debated at the time of the Protestant Reformation, concerns the interpretation of Jesus' words, 'This is my body' and 'This is my blood.' There is not space here to investigate the disagreement in any detail, but what is at stake, essentially, is whether Jesus' words entail that the bread and wine are somehow transformed so that they become the body and blood of Christ, or whether the bread and wine are rather to be interpreted as symbols of Christ's body and blood. Roman Catholic and Eastern Orthodox theologians have tended to take the first view, while giving different accounts of how the transformation takes place, and Protestant theologians have tended to adopt the second view, also with considerable variation between them about how precisely the symbolic function of the bread and wine should be understood. It must be noted that this is a simplification of a very complex debate, the details of which can be followed up elsewhere.

Amidst all the complexity of debate, however, we should not lose sight of the promise of Christ that through the breaking of bread and the sharing of wine, he will be present with his people. In the words of contemporary Lutheran theologian Robert Jenson (1930–), the bread and wine are means through which Christ makes himself available to us (see Jenson, *Systematic Theology*, vol. 2, pp. 250–59). These created realities of bread and wine, 'fruit of the earth and work of human hands', as the Roman Catholic liturgy puts it, become vehicles of the divine presence. It is for this reason that the Lord's Supper is called a sacrament. A sacrament is a created reality that is made, through the indwelling of the Spirit, a vehicle for God's presence and action in the world. Susan Ross explains that a sacrament 'expresses God's amazing presence in human life, the potential of all life to reveal God's presence, and the importance of relating the hospitality of God's gracious love in every possible dimension of human life' ('Church and Sacrament, Community and Worship', p. 235). It is worth noting as well, as has been done by Colin Gunton in *The Christian Faith* (p. 134), that through divine use of these fruits of the earth, the wider created world is representatively incorporated into communion with God. Here is to be found, Gunton suggests, the basis for an ecological ethic. The true end towards which creation is directed is to be taken up into praise of the Creator. That is a rather different vision of the value of creation than is entailed by its exploitation solely for human ends.

Certain implications for human social ethics are also powerfully present in the celebration of the Lord's Supper. In Christian thought, the breaking of bread is regarded as a representation of the death of Jesus. This interpretation suggests itself clearly enough and certainly forms part of the theological significance of the breaking of bread, but in the Passover meal the main emphasis of the division was on sharing out the blessing of God. Those who share bread are bound together as one people under God's blessing. It is for this reason that outrage was expressed when Jesus was seen eating with outcasts and sinners. In so doing, he made them one with himself, and he one with them. He broke down the customary social divisions and established fellowship with those who were despised and ostracised. That the Lord's Supper creates a bond among those who share in it and overcomes social divisions of all kinds is emphasised in Paul's interpretative comment on the Lord's Supper: 'Because there is one bread, we who are many are one body; for we all share in the one bread' (1 Corinthians 10:17). It is for this reason too that Paul is outraged by the continuation of social divisions among the Christians in Corinth when they gather to celebrate the Lord's Supper (see 1 Corinthians 11:17–34). The sharing of bread at the Lord's Supper exemplifies the eradication of divisions based on gender, social class, ethnicity, culture, economic status and so on, that is, or should be, a feature of the new community established in Christ.

WORSHIP

Acts 2 reports that, following Pentecost, the first Christians spent much time in prayer and in praising God. The practice of worship is not merely one feature of Christian community alongside others, but the very heart of new life in Christ. Worship takes place as we enter with Christ and in the power of the Spirit into the reality of reconciled relationship with God and with neighbour. To put the matter as James Torrance (1923–2003) has done, worship is the gift of 'participation through the Spirit in the Son's communion with the Father' (Torrance, *Worship, Community and the Triune God of Grace*). Torrance goes on to point out that worship, considered in this way, is not really something that we do, but rather something that we are drawn into by the Spirit. Paul, in his letter to the Romans, puts it this way:

> For all who are led by the Spirit of God are children of God. For you did not receive a spirit of slavery to fall back into fear, but you have received a spirit of adoption. When we cry, 'Abba! Father!' it is that very Spirit bearing witness with our spirit that we are children of God, and if children, then heirs, heirs of God and joint heirs with Christ (Romans 8:14–17) … Likewise the Spirit helps us in our weakness; for we do not know how to pray as we ought, but that very Spirit intercedes with sighs too deep for words. And God, who searches the heart, knows what is the mind of the Spirit, because the Spirit intercedes for the saints according to the will of God.
>
> (Romans 8:26–27)

Sarah Coakley (1951–) observes that Paul offers here a thoroughly Trinitarian understanding of what happens in Christian prayer. God is simultaneously doing the praying in me (as the Spirit), receiving that prayer (as the Father) and inviting me into Christ's life of redeemed sonship ('The Trinity, Prayer and Sexuality', pp. 260–61). Coakley here repeats Paul's language of sonship, but, as Paul makes clear elsewhere, the reality of the redeemed children of God involves both male and female. Following Coakley's Pauline lead, we may say that worship is that gift by which we are drawn into the life of the living God, a life characterised above all by love. To be drawn into that life is to participate also in God's love for the world. That is why, in Micah 6:8, worship is very closely connected with love and service of one's neighbour. In contemplating what offering he might bring to worship God, the prophet declares, 'He has told you O mortal what is good; and what does the Lord require of you but to do justice, and to love kindness, and to walk humbly with your God.'

There is, unfortunately, a widespread misconception among Christians that worship is simply the singing of songs of praise. The biblical understanding of worship involves much more than that.

Worship consists in the devotion of one's whole life to God. When Christians gather together to give thanks to God, to offer praise, to attend to the Word of God, to share together in the Lord's Supper and to offer prayers for one another and for the world, their worship in this way is a concentrated and explicit expression of what should be true of one's whole life.

A further misconception about worship, perhaps even more widespread, is that worship involves telling God how wonderful he is, and expressing our grateful thanks for all that God has done. There will be occasion for such sentiments to be expressed in worship but, again, the Bible offers a much broader conception of what worship involves. In the Psalms, for instance, a vast range of sentiments is expressed, including lamentation, anger, protest and even vengeance. Consider, for example, Psalm 58 or the notorious Psalm 157, both of which express bitter anger and a desire for revenge against Israel's enemies. We might suppose that such sentiments have no place in worship, but the outrage and bitter anguish of the Psalmist is uttered in protest against the destruction of Jerusalem and the slaughter of many of its inhabitants. Outrage ought to be expressed in response to such evil. The alternatives are to condone it, or to be indifferent. It is appropriate to bring such things before God in prayer. Dietrich Bonhoeffer has pointed out, however, that whoever brings their anger and their vengeance before God waives the right to seek vengeance themselves (see Kuske, *The Old Testament as the Book of Christ*, p. 86). 'Vengeance is mine', says the Lord, and 'I will repay' (Romans 12:19; cf. Deuteronomy 32:35). The Psalmist brings to God his outrage at what has been perpetrated by Israel's enemies and pleads with God that justice will be done. In response to the Psalmist's anguished cry, the Bible affirms that God will execute justice, but, as we have seen in chapter five, God's justice turns out to be different from our own. The justice of God is exercised on the cross, where God takes humanity's sin and evil upon himself in order to heal and forgive and reconcile. Those who take all aspects of their lives to God in worship and in prayer are liable to discover by doing so a different way of being. That is precisely what was being discovered as, in the early church, the first Christians 'devoted themselves to the apostles' teaching and fellowship, to the breaking of bread and the prayers' (Acts 2:42).

Dietrich Bonhoeffer (1906–45) was a German theologian who was executed just before the end of the Second World War on account of his opposition to Hitler.

A COMMON LIFE

A notable feature of the new way of being discovered by the first Christians is described in the same passage that we have been considering in Acts 2: 'All who believed were together and had all things in common; they would sell their possessions and goods and distribute the proceeds to all, as any had need' (Acts 2:44–45). These Christians saw clearly that the Christian gospel entails a radical reordering of our social and economic life. That different form of social and economic life is presented in Acts 2 as a distinctive mark of the Christian community. It should be noted that the focus in these verses on social and economic transformation is not exceptional in the New Testament. We have already made reference to Paul's insistence that those who share together in the Lord's Supper should abandon all divisions based on social class and economic standing. There are, in addition, numerous other passages in both the Old and New Testaments of the Bible that stress God's concern for the poor and the oppressed. Paul seems to insist that any Christian community that allows social and economic injustice to continue among its members is failing to live according to the new reality of God's coming kingdom.

As was mentioned briefly in chapter one, it has taken the work of theologians working in the slums of Latin America and Asia to remind wealthy Christians in the Western world that care for the poor and liberation of the oppressed are not marginal issues in the Bible. One of the great pioneers of liberation theology, Gustavo Gutiérrez (1928–), has written, 'One must keep in mind that the God of the Bible is a God who not only governs history, but who orients it in the direction of establishment of justice and right. He is more than a provident God. He is a God who takes sides with the poor and liberates them from slavery and oppression' (*The Power of the Poor in History*, p. 7). Well versed in Jewish Scripture, the first Christians apparently had no doubt that the liberating power of the gospel had clear social, economic and political implications.

The church in the West has a long history, developed especially through the monastic tradition in the Middle Ages, of building hospitals and almshouses, of caring for the sick and the poor, and of providing hospitality to strangers, and it remains the case that in many Western countries the vast majority of social service agencies and foreign aid organisations have Christian roots, even if not all have retained a distinctly Christian understanding of their work. For all the good that is done through such organisations, the way of Jesus demands more than charitable giving at arm's length. A financial donation to the poor given without any personal contact falls short of the picture painted in Acts 2, in which the first Christians 'had all things in common', broke bread and prayed together, and distributed their possessions to all who had need. The Bible repeatedly suggests that Christian discipleship demands a radical transformation of oppressive and unjust social and economic structures, but at the heart of that transformation is a new form of community in which strangers are welcomed, the poor are given seats of honour at the Lord's table, lepers are embraced, sinners are forgiven, the needs of all are met and the dignity of all as beloved children of God is upheld and celebrated. Finding ways to respond to that biblical imperative in widely divergent cultural, political and economic contexts remains an urgent task for the church today.

FORMS OF MINISTRY

One of the things that is made very clear in the apostle Paul's writings on the church is that everybody who is part of the church, or part of 'the Body of Christ', as Paul calls it, has a role to play within it. Perhaps the most well-known passage in which Paul insists on this point is 1 Corinthians 12. Paul describes various gifts that are given for the building up of the body and for the exercise of ministry. These include wisdom and understanding, healing, prophecy, tongues, helping others, teaching, prayer and so on. Paul makes two very important points about these gifts. The first is that they are all gifts of the Spirit and are given 'for the common good' (1 Corinthians 12:7). They are not to be used for individual advancement or as a cause of boasting. Rather, they are to be used in service of the whole body. The second point is that while some gifts don't seem to be quite as spectacular as others, all are necessary and equally valuable. This is the point of Paul's famous passage concerning the members of the body: 'As it is, there are many members, yet one body. The eye cannot say to the hand, "I have no need of you", nor again the head to the feet, "I have no need of you"', and so on (1 Corinthians 12:20–21). All the members of the body are needed and have a part to play. Theologians during the Protestant Reformation placed particular emphasis on this Pauline account and insisted that all Christians are made ministers by virtue of their baptism.

Paul's emphasis on the church as the Body of Christ, and his instruction about the gifts of the Spirit being given variously to all members of the body, indicate that the church is a community gathered by Christ and equipped by the Spirit working in its midst. Yet the church is also a human institution and has adopted certain forms and rules in order to organise its life and assist it to remain faithful to its divine calling. The New Testament gives some guidance on particular roles of leadership and service that are important in the church, but nowhere does it offer a detailed design for the organisation of the church as an institution. Churches have therefore evolved and adapted the forms of leadership that appear at different times to have been necessary in order for the church to have shared faithfully in the mission of God. Predominant among the forms of leadership, however, have been the roles of the ordained minister or priest, the role of the bishop and the role of the elder. The particular tasks of the priest or minister are conceived a little differently across various branches of the church, but they commonly involve preaching, leading the celebration of the sacraments and providing pastoral care. Priests and ministers are usually ordained to undertake these responsibilities. Ordination involves the priest or minister being suitably prepared to undertake these tasks through a programme of training and Christian formation, being approved by the church to do so and being commissioned through a special service of ordination to the role of priest or minister. Such commissioning services include as a central feature prayer and the laying on of hands. As prayers are said, ministers, priests and bishops, in some churches, lay their hands on the shoulders of the person being ordained, thus representing symbolically that he or she is part of a long line of people commissioned and authorised to proclaim the gospel through the preaching of the gospel and the celebration of the sacraments. The person being ordained is part of a tradition of ministerial leadership originating with the apostles, and is now made responsible for faithfully carrying that tradition forward. They undertake this task with the blessing and support of the church as a whole.

Despite particular people being ordained to undertake these tasks of preaching, celebration of the sacraments and pastoral care, most churches recognise that preaching and pastoral care is also undertaken very faithfully by those who are not ordained. It is usually only the celebration of the sacraments that is reserved for ordained priests or ministers. This is because the sacraments are a symbolic enactment of the very heart of the gospel and the church has considered it necessary, by appointing particular people to the task, to ensure that the sacraments are administered with due care.

Consistent with Paul's emphasis upon the interdependence of the members of the Body of Christ, churches have developed structures of accountability and support that reflect that interdependence. In many churches, including Roman Catholic, Lutheran, Orthodox, Anglican and Episcopalian, among some others, the unity and interdependence of the church is expressed through the office of the bishop. A bishop has oversight of the church in a particular region, while national and international oversight of the church is provided through the office of archbishop, and, in the case of the Roman Catholic Church, through the Pope, who is also the bishop of Rome. The bishops are a focus for unity in the church and connect the local church to the national and international community of the Body of Christ.

In Reformed churches, however, the structure of the church is less hierarchical. The accountability of ministers and the interdependence of churches is provided through the office of the elder. In the Presbyterian system of church government, for example, the ordained minister of word and sacrament is known as a 'teaching elder' and shares responsibility for spiritual leadership of the local church with 'ruling elders'. The gathering of ministers and elders at a regional level is called a Presbytery, while the highest 'court' of the church is the General Assembly, a national gathering of minsters and elders. Authority rests with the gathered community of elders and ministers, rather than with a single officeholder, as in the case of bishops.

A third common form of church structure is the congregational form. Adopted by Baptists and by many independent churches, authority in churches of this type rests with the local congregation. Such churches often enter into fellowship with other churches and form a union of similar churches, but they reserve the right to make their own final decisions about the life of their own congregation.

It can be argued that each of these common forms has its strengths and its weaknesses. Theologically understood, however, it is important that churches find ways to remain faithful to Paul's vision of the church as a body in which all members have their part to play in sharing together in the work of God's people, and that it find some means of expressing the unity of the church as a whole. There can be, after all, only one 'body of Christ'. The fragmentation of the Christian church remains an unfortunate reality that fails to bear effective witness to the unity of Christians, who are supposed to have one Lord, one faith and one baptism.

THE ONE, HOLY, CATHOLIC AND APOSTOLIC CHURCH

In the Nicene Creed, one of the classic statements of Christian belief, the church confesses, 'We believe in one, holy, catholic and apostolic church.' This is a theological claim, rather than a sociological one. At a sociological level, or, we might say, in what appears to the onlooker, it is clear that the church is not one body. It is divided and fragmented. Nor is it particularly holy, if by the term 'holy' we mean that it is transparent to the holiness of God. The term 'catholic' means, in this context, universal, which is to say that the church is for all people. It can never be exclusive. And yet, there are times when in particular places the church is found to be exclusive. A 'church' segregated on racial lines, for instance, exists in denial of the catholicity of the church. A 'church' in which gay people are not welcome, or a 'church' in which people of a different social class are made to feel awkward and out of place, or a 'church' from which people with disabilities are excluded through neglect of their particular needs falls short of the call to be the church for all people. It fails to be catholic.

The term 'apostolic' also needs some explanation. It has a dual sense. As the contemporary German theologian Jürgen Moltmann (1926–) has put it, for the church to be apostolic means that

> ... its gospel and its doctrine are founded on the testimony of the first apostles, the eyewitnesses of the risen Christ, and it exists in the carrying out of the apostolic proclamation, the missionary charge. The expression 'apostolic' therefore denotes both the church's foundation and its commission.

> *(The Church in the Power of the Spirit*, p. 358)

With respect to both these features, the church, in a sociological sense, manages to be apostolic only in fits and starts. There are times when its proclamation in word and deed is only remotely related, if at all, to the good news proclaimed by the apostles, and there are times when its energies are devoted to things other than the missionary imperative to make known the gospel through proclamation and in service to the world.

What does it mean, then, for the church to confess, 'We believe in one, holy, catholic and apostolic church'? It means, first of all, that these attributes of unity, holiness, catholicity and apostolicity describe the church's true identity. To be sure, these attributes describe what the church is called to be, but is not yet in its fullness. And so the church must continue to repent of its failings, and continue to seek the guidance and the enabling of the Spirit to make it what it is called to be. But these attributes also describe what can be uttered only in faith, that the dishevelled, fragmented, hypocritical and stumbling people who gather at local churches all around the world are, despite all appearances, the one Body of Christ. United to Christ by the Spirit and so also to one another, they are appointed to be bearers of the gospel in the world. That divine calling and appointment is the basis of the church's unity. There is only one Lord, who is the head of the church, and only one Body of Christ into which Christians are incorporated through baptism. The holiness of the church, also confessed as a matter of faith, consists in the fact that God makes use of the church despite its many weaknesses. God sets it apart and makes it an instrument of his good and holy purposes for the world. The church's catholicity, theologically understood, consists in the fact that the church's Lord and the one to whom the church bears witness invites all to come to him, and is, through the Spirit, continually forming and reforming the church so that the gospel may be heard in many languages and find expression in widely divergent cultural contexts. Finally, the apostolicity of the church is sustained by the Spirit who, in spite of the church's multiple failings, preserves the gospel in its midst and gathers the church again and again to participate in Christ's mission to reconcile all things to the Father.

The church is, perpetually, a work in progress. Just as God does not wait upon individuals to become perfect before he calls them to be his witnesses, so too he does not wait upon the perfection of the church before it too becomes a witness to the gracious and redemptive love of God for the world. The church can easily be criticised. Its failings are obvious. But God has no other people to work with than sinful and imperfect people. As the biblical story repeatedly shows, there is no other kind available.

Before concluding this chapter on the new community, we return once more to the formation of the church on the day of Pentecost. Acts 2 reports that when the Sprit came upon the people, all who were there heard the Spirit-inspired words spoken in their own languages (Acts 2:1–11). There were Parthians, Medes, Elamites and residents of Mesopotamia, Judea and Cappadocia, Pontus and Asia, and so on. The multiplicity of languages and the diversity of cultures represented is, as has been mentioned earlier, a dramatic extension of God's promise to 'all nations'. This extension of the divine promise has important implications for the life of the church and for theology. Both the church as a community, and the thinking the church does about the gospel that has been entrusted to it, are to be enriched by a multiplicity of voices and cultures. The introduction to theology offered in this book is dominated by a Western and a male perspective, but a reminder is offered here that many voices contribute to the theological enterprise and serve to enrich, extend and correct, as needed, the theological insights emerging from all quarters of the church's life. Male and female, rich and poor, Asian and African, Latin American and Polynesian cultures and voices, to name but a few, all have contributions to make to the task of exploring and articulating the new reality that God is bringing about, and of reforming the worldwide church so that it may remain faithful in ever-changing times to the good news of God's creative and redemptive purposes for the world.

FOR FURTHER READING

The work of the Spirit in forming and equipping the church can be explored further in Jürgen Moltmann, *The Church in the Power of the Spirit* (London: SCM Press, 1977), and in Simon Chan, *Liturgical Theology: The Church as Worshipping Community* (Downers Grove, IL: InterVarsity Press, 2006). General discussions of the church, each with particular emphases, can be found in Jon Sobrino, *The True Church and the Poor* (London: SCM Press, 1984), Letty Russell, *Church in the Round: Feminist Interpretation of the Church* (Louisville, KY: Westminster John Knox Press, 1993), Hans Küng, *The Church* (London: Search Press, 1968), and William H. Willimon, *What's Right with the Church* (San Francisco: Harper and Row, 1989).

Further discussions of the sacraments are provided in Alasdair I. C. Heron, *Table and Tradition: Toward an Ecumenical Understanding of the Eucharist* (Philadelphia: Westminster Press, 1983), World Council of Churches, *Baptism, Eucharist and Ministry* (Geneva: World Council of Churches, 1982), and Susan Ross, 'Church and Sacrament, Community and Worship', in *The Cambridge Companion to Feminist Theology*, edited by Susan Frank Parsons (Cambridge: Cambridge University Press, 2002), 224–42.

GLOSSARY

Age of Reason A term coined by Thomas Paine, indicating the era roughly spanning the seventeenth and eighteenth centuries during which human reason was thought to be triumphant over the traditional authorities of Scripture and church.

Anabaptist A movement from sixteenth-century Europe that sought radical reformation of the church. It survives in various forms today, notably in the Mennonite church. Anabaptism means to baptise again, after the practice of re-baptising those who joined the movement from other churches.

Apologists Theologians of the second century who sought to give a reasoned defence of Christian faith in dialogue with Greek philosophy.

apostles The first disciples of Jesus, along with Saint Paul.

Apostles' Creed An early statement of Christian belief probably dating from the second century but whose origins are uncertain. It is widely recognised by churches throughout the world.

apostolic Refers both to the tradition of faith deriving from the apostles, and to the church's calling to proclaim the gospel in word and deed.

Arianism A belief originating with Arius in the fourth century that the Son is not fully divine, and is not co-eternal with the Father.

atonement Refers to the reconciliation with God brought about through the overcoming of human sin.

baptism A rite of initiation into the Christian faith through which the baptised person is cleansed of sin, is united with Christ in his death and resurrection and is made one with the Body of Christ, the church.

beatific vision Refers to the hope that one day the believer will see God face to face in all his glory.

blasphemy The act of showing contempt for God or for something sacred.

Book of Common Prayer A book of prayers and other texts for use in services of worship in the Anglican Church. Its first edition dates from 1549.

catholic Regarded as an attribute of the church, catholic means universal or 'for all'.

catechism A manual of instruction in Christian doctrine usually taking the form of a series of questions and answers. Until relatively recently, candidates for baptism were expected to learn a catechism by heart. There are numerous catechisms prepared by different branches of the church.

Charismatic Refers to the gifts or 'charisma' given by the Spirit for the upbuilding of the church and the strengthening of faith. The Charismatic movement developed during the twentieth century placed a particular emphasis upon such gifts, particularly speaking in tongues and prophecy.

Copernican Revolution The revolution in thought and culture brought about by the discovery by Copernicus (1473–1543) that the sun rather than Earth lies at the centre of the solar system.

cosmos aisthetos The temporal and material world that human beings inhabit, and thought by classical Greek philosophers to be a shadowy and imperfect reflection of the real world of immaterial forms or ideas.

cosmos noetos The intelligible and eternal world of pure ideas, thought by Greek philosophers to be the real world.

Council of Chalcedon A major church Council that met in 451 and affirmed both the true humanity and the true divinity of Christ.

Council of Trent A Council of the Roman Catholic Church that met between 1545 and 1563 that clarified and reaffirmed the teaching of the Roman Catholic Church in response to the Protestant Reformation.

covenant An unconditional commitment binding two parties together in mutual relationship. The relationship that God has with his people is repeatedly referred to in the Bible as a covenant.

creatio ex nihilo Creation out of nothing.

creed A formal statement of belief deriving from the Latin 'credo', meaning 'I believe'.

deistic The belief that God created the world but, having determined the laws by which the universe will operate, then left it to its own devices.

demiurge A figure originating in Platonic philosophy and taken up by Gnosticism, indicating a craftsman-like figure who is responsible for making the universe.

divine economy Refers to the work done by God in and for the world. The economic being of God is distinguished from the immanent being of God, the latter referring to God's being in himself, apart from his relation to the world.

Docetism The belief, regarded as heretical, that Christ was truly divine but only appeared to be human.

doctrine Refers to the teaching of the church or to that collection of theological beliefs considered to be central to Christian faith.

Eastern Orthodox The church tradition stemming from the Greek-speaking, eastern parts of the Roman Empire. The Eastern church divided from the Western, predominantly Latin-speaking, church in the eleventh century.

Ebionitism The belief, regarded as heretical, that Christ was truly human and an inspired teacher of the law but was not divine.

Enlightenment A major cultural shift that took place in seventeenth-century Europe and in which human reason and scientific enquiry were increasingly regarded as the most reliable means of learning the truth.

episcopal Pertaining to the ecclesiastical office of bishop.

eschatology That branch of theology concerned with the study of the last things or with the final goal and end of history.

evangelism The practice of spreading and proclaiming the good news of the Christian gospel.

feminism A movement and set of ideas devoted to affirming the equal rights of women with men and seeking to overcome all forms of prejudice and practice that belittle, oppress or disadvantage women.

Gnosticism Refers to a cluster of ideas that developed in the first and second centuries AD, and stressed the need to attain an esoteric knowledge (gnosis) in order to attain salvation. Gnosticism typically privileges the spiritual realm over the material world and regards the latter as the realm of evil and sin.

Hellenistic Refers to the system of thought and culture originating in ancient Greece that became widely influential throughout the Roman Empire.

hypostasis In the context of theology, this Greek term is usually translated as person. It is used for the three persons of the Trinity.

idolatry The practice of worshipping something other than God.

immutability The attribute of constancy and unchangeability. When used of God, it refers to the utter reliability and trustworthiness of the God who is the same, yesterday, today and forever.

incarnation Refers to the event in which the eternal Son of God becomes flesh and takes upon himself our humanity.

justification The divine action in which sinners are forgiven and are restored to right relationship with God.

kenosis A Greek word meaning 'emptying', sometimes used to refer to the self-emptying of the Son of God as he becomes human or as he takes the lowly form of a servant.

kingdom of God A biblical term used to refer to the coming reign of God in which the world is ordered according to God's purpose.

lex orandi, lex credendi 'The law (or rule) of praying is the law (or rule) of believing'. The phrase is used in theology to indicate that Christian belief is fostered by a life of prayer and worship.

liberal theology This term can be used for a very broad range of Christian positions but is used particularly of the theology that developed in nineteenth-century Europe and that tended to emphasise the teaching and ethics of Jesus while downplaying the church's traditional claims about his divinity.

liberation theology A widely influential movement developed during the second half of the twentieth century, especially in Latin America, that emphasises the attention given in the Bible to God's care for the poor and God's concern to liberate the downtrodden and the oppressed.

liturgy The form and content of Christian worship.

Lord's Supper The re-enactment in the context of Christian worship of the meal that Jesus shared with his disciples prior to his crucifixion. Also known as the Mass, the Eucharist and Holy Communion.

Messiah God's anointed one. Originated with the expectation in ancient Israel that one day God would anoint a chosen one to bring to fulfilment his purposes for Israel and for the world. 'Messiah' is a Hebrew term that is translated into Greek as 'Christ'.

metanoia A Greek term meaning the transformation of one's mind. It is usually translated in the Bible as conversion or repentance.

modalism The belief that the names Father, Son and Spirit do not refer to the three distinct divine persons but only to three modes in which the singular God appears to us. Also known as Sabellianism.

monotheism The belief that there is only one God.

Mosaic Following in the tradition of Moses.

New Atheism A name given to a particularly vociferous form of atheism developed in the last 20–30 years and which is distinguished by its insistence that religious belief, as well as being false, is the cause of widespread harm in human history. Leading exponents include Richard Dawkins, Christopher Hitchens and Sam Harris.

Nicene Creed The statement of Christian belief formulated at the Council of Nicaea in 325 and refined and formally adopted at the Council of Constantinople in 381. The Nicene Creed is commonly recited in Christian worship and is regarded as authoritative by most branches of the church throughout the world.

omnipresence The attribute of God by which God is equally present to all times and places.

omniscience The attribute of God by which God knows all things.

ordination The act of appointing and commissioning people to undertake particular tasks within the life of the Christian church, including but not limited to the ministry of preaching and the administration of the sacraments.

ousia A Greek word meaning 'being or substance', often used to speak of the one being of God.

pantheism The belief that the whole of reality is divine and that God is not distinct from but identical with the universe itself.

parousia A Greek word meaning presence or arrival, and commonly used by theologians to refer to the return of Christ.

Passover Refers to the event of God's 'passing over' the houses of the Israelites before leading them from slavery in Egypt, and to the commemorative meal celebrated every year in which Jews recall God's deliverance of their people from slavery.

Patristic theologians The theologians of the early church roughly spanning from the second to the sixth centuries and sometimes referred to as the 'church fathers'.

Pelagian The view named after the fifth-century monk Pelagius who believed, wrongly so the church has generally agreed, that human beings are capable of attaining righteousness through their own efforts and with minimal need of divine grace.

Pentecost The event reported in Acts 2 in which, following the resurrection and ascension of Jesus, the early church experienced a dramatic outpouring of the Holy Spirit.

Pentecostal A renewal movement within the church that developed during the twentieth century and that places particular emphasis on personal experience of the Holy Spirit and on the Spirit's equipping of the church to spread the gospel throughout the world.

perichoresis A Greek term used to speak of the shared life and loving interdependence of the three persons of the Trinity.

Platonic Refers to the philosophy and worldview deriving from the Greek philosopher Plato and especially to his theory of forms that affirms a realm of abstract ideas that is only imperfectly reflected in the temporal and material world of everyday existence.

pluralism Used in the context of religion, pluralism refers to the belief that the many religions represent equally valid paths to the truth.

postmodern/postmodernity Describes a culture and cluster of ideas that is currently prevalent in the Western world. While it is too diverse and disparate a culture to describe in any definitive sense, some of its distinguishing characteristics include a growing disillusionment with the confident assertions of modernity that the whole of reality could be encompassed by a single story or meta-narrative, that reason gives best access to reality itself and that human prowess and technological advance could solve our most pressing problems. Postmodern culture, in theory at least, is more accepting of difference and diversity and is reluctant to assert that there are truths that apply to all people everywhere.

process theology A form of theology developed especially in the twentieth century in which the being of God is thought to be bound up with and dependent upon the unfolding of time and history.

propitiatory sacrifice A sacrifice intended to make amends for sin.

Protestant Reformation A sixteenth-century upheaval in the church in Western Europe in which Martin Luther and others challenged accepted teachings of the church. While Luther did not set out to divide the church, the theological disputes, along with a range of political factors, eventually led to the establishment of new churches around Europe that asserted their independence from Roman Catholicism. The most important of these initially were the Lutheran Church in Germany, the Reformed Church in Switzerland and the Anglican Church in England.

Quest of the historical Jesus Prompted by the recognition of the considerable diversity in the witness of the four gospels and of the theological convictions that shaped those gospels, scholars in the nineteenth century set out to discover the so-called historical Jesus stripped bare of the theological claims that were made about him. The nineteenth-century Quest is deemed to have failed, but it has been succeeded in the twentieth century by renewed attempts to investigate the reality of Jesus using the tools of historical inquiry alone.

Reformed tradition The Reformed tradition, instigated by John Calvin, emerged from the Protestant Reformation of the sixteenth century. It is distinguished by a range of theological convictions and by a particular form of church government in which bishops and priests are replaced with a less hierarchical structure involving elders and ministers who are together responsible for the government and policy of the church.

repentance The act of sorrow and contrition in which one recognises one's sinfulness and confesses one's readiness to turn to a new way of life.

Restoration Movement A nineteenth-century reform movement in the United States that sought to return the church to the form of church life apparent in the New Testament.

Roman Catholicism The largest branch of the church globally. It is led by the Pope, who is the bishop of Rome, and traces its origins to the apostle Peter.

Romanticism A nineteenth-century intellectual, artistic and literary movement in Europe that, in reaction to the cold, unfeeling rationalism of Enlightenment culture, affirmed the value of imagination, aesthetic sensibility, feeling and emotion.

ruach A Hebrew word meaning wind, breath or spirit.

rule of faith A series of statements capturing the essentials of Christian faith and often appealed to as a guide to the reading of the Bible. There is no single definitive 'rule of faith', but particular examples can be found in the work of a number of patristic theologians.

Sabellianism See 'modalism'.

sacrament The nature of a sacrament is variously defined within different theological traditions, but involves in all traditions the celebration of a particular rite through which God makes himself present to the church. Such rites are regarded as signs of God's grace that bring into effect what they proclaim. The Lord's Supper and baptism are the two sacraments that are recognised almost universally, while some churches, including Roman Catholic and Orthodox, recognise seven sacraments.

salvation Salvation is a term that broadly describes the reality brought about through the life, death and resurrection of Jesus Christ, and that restores humanity to the form of life intended for it by God. It encompasses a range of more particular terms such as reconciliation, atonement and forgiveness.

sanctification The process of being made holy.

Scripture Literally means text, or that which is written, but in a theological context, it refers to the books of the Old and New Testaments that collectively comprise the Christian Bible.

Second Vatican Council A Council that met from 1962–65 and brought about some major reforms of the Roman Catholic Church.

Stoic Belonging to a school of Greek philosophy founded in Athens in the third century BC, the distinguishing mark of which was the quest for moral and intellectual perfection attained in part by freeing oneself from the vagaries of emotion and by remaining calm and unperturbed by pain or misfortune.

sin Often equated with moral failing, sin is to be understood more fundamentally as the state of being alienated from God.

subordinationism The view that in the Triune being of God the Son and Spirit are subordinate to the being of the Father.

telos The end or purpose of a thing.

tertium quid A 'third thing', often indicating 'neither one thing nor the other'. The term is used of Arius' view of Jesus, which portrays Jesus as neither fully divine nor fully human.

theodicy The study of the problem of evil and suffering and the attempt to reconcile the reality of evil and suffering with the existence of a good and all-powerful God.

Thirty-Nine Articles A definitive statement of the doctrine and beliefs of the Anglican Church, first drafted in 1563.

tritheism The belief that there are three gods. Usually contrasted with the Trinitarian belief that Father, Son and Spirit are three persons in one God.

BIBLIOGRAPHY

Abelard, Peter, 'Exposition of the Epistle to the Romans II', in *A Scholastic Miscellany: Anselm to Ockham*, Library of Christian Classics (London: SCM Press, 1956).

Anselm, *Cur Deus Homo* (Edinburgh: John Grant, 1909).

——, *The Prayers and Meditations of St Anselm* (Harmondsworth, UK: Penguin Classics, 1973).

Appiah-Kubi, Kofi, 'Christology', in J. Mbiti, ed., *African and Asian Contributions to Contemporary Theology* (Geneva: Ecumenical Institute, 1976).

Augustine, *Reply to Faustus the Manichaean*, in *Nicene and Post-Nicene Fathers*, First series, vol. 4, ed. Philip Schaff (Buffalo, NY: Christian Literature Publishing, 1887).

——, *On the Holy Trinity*, in *Nicene and Post-Nicene Fathers*, First series, vol. 3, ed. Philip Schaff (Buffalo, NY: Christian Literature Publishing, 1887).

Aulen, Gustav, *Christus Victor* (New York: Macmillan, 1931).

Barth, Karl, *Church Dogmatics*, 4 vols. (Edinburgh: T&T Clark, 1936–62).

Bauckham, Richard, 'Eschatology', in *The Oxford Handbook of Systematic Theology*, eds John Webster, Kathryn Tanner and Iain Torrance (Oxford: Oxford University Press, 2007), 306–22.

Berry, R. J., ed., *The Care of Creation: Focussing Concern and Action* (Leicester: Inter-Varsity Press, 2000).

——, ed., *Environmental Stewardship: Critical Perspectives Past and Present* (London: T&T Clark, 2006).

Bockmuehl, Markus, ed., *The Cambridge Companion to Jesus* (Cambridge: Cambridge University Press, 2001).

Boesak, Allan Aubrey, *Farewell to Innocence: A Socio-Ethical Study on Black Theology and Black Power* (Maryknoll, NY: Orbis Books, 1977).

Boff, Leonardo, and Clodovis Boff, *Introducing Liberation Theology* (Tunbridge Wells, UK: Burns and Oates, 1987).

Breuggemann, Walter, *Genesis: Interpretation: A Bible Commentary for Teaching and Preaching* (Atlanta: John Knox Press, 1982).

Buckley, Michael, *At the Origins of Modern Atheism* (New Haven, CT: Yale University Press, 1990).

Burridge, Richard, *Four Gospels, One Jesus*, 2nd ed. (Grand Rapids, MI: Eerdmans, 2005).

Bynum, Caroline Walker, *Jesus as Mother: Studies in the Spirituality of the High Middle Ages* (Berkeley: University of California Press, 1982).

Calvin, John, *Institutes of the Christian Religion*, ed. John T. McNeil, trans. Ford Lewis Battles (Philadelphia: Westminster Press, 1960).

Chan, Simon, *Liturgical Theology: The Church as Worshipping Community* (Downers Grove, IL: InterVarsity Press, 2006).

Coakley, Sarah, 'The Trinity, Prayer and Sexuality', in *Feminism and Theology*, eds Janet Martin Soskice and Diana Lipton (Oxford: Oxford University Press, 2003), 258–67.

Daly, Mary, *Beyond God the Father: Toward a Philosophy of Women's Liberation* (Boston: Beacon, 1973).

D'Costa, Gavin, 'The Impossibility of a Pluralist View of Religions', in *Religious Studies* 32.2 (June 1996), 223–32.

Dostoyevsky, Fyodor, *The Brothers Karamazov* (London: Penguin Books, 1983).

Fergusson, David, 'Creation', in *The Oxford Handbook of Systematic Theology*, eds John Webster, Kathryn Tanner and Iain Torrance (Oxford: Oxford University Press, 2007), 72–90.

Fiddes, Paul, 'Salvation', in *The Oxford Handbook of Systematic Theology*, eds John Webster, Kathryn Tanner and Iain Torrance (Oxford: Oxford University Press, 2007), 176–96.

Gregory of Nyssa, 'The Great Catechism', *Nicene and Post-Nicene Fathers,* series II, vol. 5, ed. Philip Schaff (Peabody, MA: Hendrickson Publishers, 1994).

Gunton, Colin E., *The Actuality of Atonement* (Edinburgh: T&T Clark, 1988).

——, *The Promise of Trinitarian Theology*, 2nd ed. (Edinburgh: T&T Clark, 1997).

——, *The Triune Creator* (Edinburgh: Edinburgh University Press, 1998).

——, *The Christian Faith: An Introduction to Christian Doctrine* (Oxford: Blackwell, 2002).

Gunton, Colin E., Stephen R. Holmes and Murray A. Rae, eds, *The Practice of Theology: A Reader* (London: SCM Press, 2001).

Gutiérrez, Gustavo, *The Power of the Poor in History* (London: SCM Press, 1983).

Haight, Roger, 'The Case for Spirit Christology', in *Theological Studies* 53.2 (1992), 257–87.

Hall, Lindsey, Murray Rae and Steve Holmes, eds, *Christian Doctrine: A Reader* (London: SCM Press, 2010).

Hart, Trevor, *Faith Thinking, The Dynamics of Christian Theology* (London: SPCK, 1995).

Hauerwas, Stanley, *The Peaceable Kingdom: A Primer in Christian Ethics* (London: SCM Press, 1983).

Held, Virginia, 'Reason, Gender and Moral Theory', in *Ethics*, ed. Peter Singer (Oxford: Oxford University Press, 1994), 166–70.

Heron, Alasdair I. C., *Table and Tradition: Toward an Ecumenical Understanding of the Eucharist* (Philadelphia: Westminster Press, 1983).

Hick, John, *Evil and the God of Love* (London: Macmillan, 1966).

Isherwood, Lisa, *Introducing Feminist Christologies* (London: Sheffield Academic Press, 2001).

Jenson, Robert, *Systematic Theology*, vol. 2 (Oxford: Oxford University Press, 1999).

Johnson, Luke Timothy, *The Real Jesus* (San Francisco: HarperCollins, 1996).

Julian of Norwich, *Revelations of Divine Love* (Mineola, NY: Dover Publications, 2006).

Karras, Valerie, 'Eschatology', in *The Cambridge Companion to Feminist Theology*, ed. Susan Frank Parsons (Cambridge: Cambridge University Press, 2002), 243–60.

Kasenene, Peter, 'Ethics in African Theology', in *Doing Ethics in Context: South African Perspectives*, eds C. Villa-Vicencio and John de Gruchy (Maryknoll, NY: Orbis Books, 1994), 138–47.

Knitter, Paul F., ed., *The Myth of Christian Uniqueness* (London: SCM Press, 1988).

Koyama, Kosuke, *No Handle on the Cross: An Asian Meditation on the Crucified Mind* (London: SCM Press, 1976).

Küng, Hans, *The Church* (London: Search Press, 1968).

Kuske, Martin, *The Old Testament as the Book of Christ: An Appraisal of Bonhoeffer's Interpretation* (Philadelphia: Westminster Press, 1976).

Kyung, Chung Hyun, *Struggle to be the Sun Again: Introducing Asian Women's Theology* (London: SCM Press, 1991).

LaCugna, Catherine Mowry, *God for Us: The Trinity and Christian Life* (San Francisco: HarperCollins, 1991).

Lewis, Alan, 'All Things New: Foundational Theses on World Mission', *Austin Seminary Bulletin* 103.4 (October 1987), 6–13.

Marguerite of Oingt, *Pagina meditationum*, in *Les oeuvres de Marguerite d'Oingt*, eds and trans Antonin Duraffour, P. Gardette and P. Durdilly (Paris: Publications de l'Institut de Linguistique Romane de Lyon 21, 1965).

McGrath, Alister E., *Christian Theology: An Introduction* (Oxford: Blackwell, 1994).

Migliore, Daniel, *Faith Seeking Understanding* (Grand Rapids, MI: Eerdmans, 1991).

Moltmann, Jürgen, *The Crucified God* (London: SCM Press, 1974).

——, *The Church in the Power of the Spirit* (London: SCM Press, 1977).

——, *The Trinity and the Kingdom: The Doctrine of God* (London: SCM Press, 1981).

——, *The Coming of God: Christian Eschatology* (London: SCM Press, 1996).

Newbigin, Lesslie, *The Gospel in a Pluralist Society* (Grand Rapids, MI: Eerdmans, 1989).

Oduyoye, Mercy Amba, 'Jesus Christ', in *The Cambridge Companion to Feminist Theology*, ed. Susan Frank Parsons (Cambridge: Cambridge University Press, 2002), 151–70.

Okure, Teresa, SHJC, 'The Global Jesus', in Markus Bockmuehl, ed., *The Cambridge Companion to Jesus* (Cambridge: Cambridge University Press, 2001), 237–49.

Parratt, John, ed., *An Introduction to Third World Theologies* (Cambridge: Cambridge University Press, 2004).

Pascal, Blaise, *Pensées* (London: Penguin, 1995).

Peacore, Linda D., *The Role of Women's Experience in Feminist Theologies of the Atonement* (Eugene, OR: Pickwick Publications, 2010).

Plantinga, Alvin, *God, Freedom and Evil* (Grand Rapids, MI: Eerdmans, 1977).

Prickett, *Romanticism and Religion: The Tradition of Coleridge and Wordsworth in the Victorian Church* (Cambridge: Cambridge University Press, 1976).

Radford Ruether, Rosemary, *To Change the World: Christology and Cultural Criticism* (London: SCM Press, 1981).

Rae, Murray, 'The Travail of God', *International Journal of Systematic Theology* 5.1 (March 2003), 47–61.

Rahner, Karl, *Foundations of Christian Faith* (London: Darton, Longman and Todd, 1978).

Ross, Susan, 'Church and Sacrament, Community and Worship', in *The Cambridge Companion to Feminist Theology*, ed. Susan Frank Parsons (Cambridge: Cambridge University Press, 2002), 224–42.

Russell, Letty, *Church in the Round: Feminist Interpretation of the Church* (Louisville, KY: Westminster John Knox Press, 1993).

Sanders, Fred, 'The Trinity', in *Mapping Modern Theology: A Thematic and Historical Introduction*, eds Kelly M. Kapic and Bruce L. McCormack (Grand Rapids, MI: Baker Academic, 2012), 21–45.

Shakespeare, William, *Macbeth* (London: Methuen, 1964).

Smail, Tom, *Once and for All: A Confession of the Cross* (London: Darton, Longman & Todd, 1998).

Sobrino, Jon, *The True Church and the Poor* (London: SCM Press, 1984).

Soskice, Janet Martin, 'Trinity and Feminism', in *The Cambridge Companion to Feminist Theology*, ed. Susan Frank Parsons (Cambridge: Cambridge University Press, 2002), 135–50.

Stanton, Graham N., *The Gospels and Jesus*, 2nd ed. (Oxford: Oxford University Press, 2002).

Surin, Kenneth, *Theology and the Problem of Evil* (Oxford: Blackwell, 1986).

Tertullian, *On Repentance in Ante-Nicene Fathers*, vol. 3 (Peabody, MA: Hendrickson, 1994).

Torrance, James B., 'Covenant or Contract? A Study of the Theological Background of Worship in Seventeenth-Century Scotland', in *Scottish Journal of Theology* 23 (1970), 51–76.

——, *Worship, Community and the Triune God of Grace* (Downers Grove, IL: InterVarsity Press, 1996).

Torrance, Thomas F., *Atonement: The Person and Work of Christ*, ed. Robert T. Walker (Downers Grove, IL: InterVarsity Press, 2009).

Turretin, Francis, *The Institutes of Elenctic Theology* (Phillipsburg, NJ: P&R Publishing, 1992).

Walker, Alice, *The Color Purple* (New York: Washington Square Press, 1982).

White, Lynn Townsend Jr, 'The Historical Roots of Our Ecologic Crisis', *Science* 155.3767 (March 10, 1967), 1203–7.

Wiesel, Elie, *A Jew Today* (New York: Random House, 1978).

Willimon, William H., *What's Right with the Church* (San Francisco: Harper and Row, 1989).

Wilson Kastner, Patricia, *Faith, Feminism and the Christ* (Philadelphia: Fortress Press, 1983).

Witvliet, Theo, *The Way of the Black Messiah* (London: SCM Press, 1987).

Wolterstorff, Nicholas, *Lament for a Son* (Grand Rapids, MI: Eerdmans, 1987).

World Council of Churches, *Baptism, Eucharist and Ministry* (Geneva: World Council of Churches, 1982).

Wright, N. T., *Who Was Jesus?* (Grand Rapids, MI: Eerdmans, 1993).

Zikmund, Barbara Brown, 'The Trinity and Women's Experience', in *Christian Century* (April 15, 1987), 354–56.

Zizioulas, John, *Being as Communion* (New York: St Vladimir's Seminary Press, 1985).

INDEX

Abelard, P. 107–8
Anselm 99, 103, 105–6, 109
anti-semitism 49
Apollinarius 63
Apologists 14
Apostles' Creed 3
apostolic 12, 157; tradition 59
Appiah-Kubi, K. 67–68
Aquinas, T. 15
Arianism 59–63
Aristides 14
Arius 59–62, 76–77, 81
ascension 111, 140
Athanasius 60–62, 77
atonement 98, 99, 100, 102, 104–6,
    107
Augustine 79, 104
Aulen, G. 101

baptism 145–46, 154, 156
Barth, K. 38, 82–83, 84, 101, 132
Basil of Caesarea 78, 119
Basilides 33
Bauckham, R. 128
beatific vision 121
Bhagavad Gita 130

Big Bang Theory 26
body of Christ 144, 154–55, 157
Boesak, A.A. 67
Boethius 40
Bonhoeffer, D. 151–52
Borodin, A. 135–36
Breuggemann, W. 90
Buckley, M. 82
Bultmann, R. 53

Calvin, J. 5, 11, 16, 107
Campbell, A. 12
Campbell, J.M. 104
Cappadocian Fathers 78
Charismatic Movement 68
Christ 3, 31, 36, 52, 53, 56, 62, 65,
    67, 80, 107, 110, 145, 148;
    example of 108; as Saviour 61,
    102–5; natures of 63–65, 76–77;
    return of 132–33; uniqueness of
    132; see also Jesus
church 5, 13, 20, 68, 78, 142–43,
    145, 156–58; tradition of the 7–12
Clement of Alexandria 14, 15
Coakley, S. 150
Cobb, J.B. 27

Cone, J. 67
Constantine 60
conversion 49
Copernican Revolution 13
Council of Chalcedon 10, 63, 64
Council of Constantinople 62,
  63, 77
Council of Ephesus 63
Council of Nicaea 60, 62, 64, 76–77
Council of Trent 9
covenant 37–38, 71–72
creation 23–25, 133, 134, 149;
  out of nothing 26–27, 38;
  telos of 27
Cyprian 105

Daly, M. 20, 85
Dawkins, R. 17
Deism 30
Descartes, R. 13, 40
divine economy 2
Docetism 57–58
Dodd, C.H. 114
dominion 30–31, 35
Dostoyevsky, F. 125

Ebionitism 58
Enlightenment 13
Epicurus 123
eschatology 113–14
eternal life 120–21
Eutyches 63
evil 123–28
evolution 24
experience 17–22

faith 4, 14, 15, 32, 54, 112,
  143, 157
feminist theology 19, 20, 84–87

Galileo 13
Gnosticism 33
God: as Father 86–87; glory of
  133–36; grace of 104, 106; love of
  38, 104, 127, 134, 150; sovereignty
  of 26; travail of 109–10

Gregory Nazianzus 78, 99
Gregory of Nyssa 78, 99
Gunton, C.E. 82, 102, 145,
  148–49
Gutiérrez, G. 20–21, 152

Harris, S. 17
Hartshorne, C. 27
heaven 122–23
Hegel, G.W.F. 52
hell 122–23
Hick, J. 64, 125–26, 129–30, 131
history 119
Hitchens, C. 17
Hubmaier, B. 12
human being 38, 41
humanity 66, 90–92
Hume, D. 123

image of God 35–37
immortality 120
incarnation 29
Irenaeus 10, 30, 33, 59,
  75–76, 119
Israel 1, 2, 6, 32, 37, 49, 50–51,
  71–72, 129, 142, 147

Jenson, R. 148
Jeremias, J. 114
Jesus 43, 44–52, 66–68, 117;
  baptism of 58, 65, 96–97; death
  of 97, 99; divinity of 56, 58–59,
  60, 62, 63, 66; humanity of 45,
  55, 58–59, 63
judgement 71–72, 107, 128–29
Julian of Norwich 109
justice 106–7, 151
justification 106–7
Justin Martyr 14

Kähler, M. 54
Kant, I. 13, 53, 108
Karras, V. 86
Käsemann, E. 53
Kasenene, P. 41
Keble, J. 18

kenosis 65
Kierkegaard, S.A. 47
King, M.L. 67
kingdom of God 44, 48, 113, 114, 115, 116–18, 152
Kitamori, K. 67
Koyama, K. 67

LaCugna, C.M. 84
language 4, 84–87
Laplace, P-S. 34
Lewis, A. 132
liberation theology 19, 20–21
Lord's supper 146–49, 151
Luther, M. 9, 16, 106

Marguerite of Oingt 109–10
McFague, S. 115
Messiah 45, 48, 49–51
metanoia 33
ministry 153–56
mission 33, 97, 101, 132, 139, 143, 144, 154, 157, 158
modalism 74, 79, 81
Moltmann, J. 157
monotheism 62, 70

Nestorius 63
New Atheism 17
new creation 113
Nicene Creed 3, 62

ordination 154
Origen 99

Pannenberg W. 53
parousia 133
Pascal, B. 17
passover 147, 149
Pelagian 108
Pentecost 140–42, 143, 158
Pentecostal 68
perichoresis 78
Philoponus 81
Plantinga, A. 126

Plato 32, 120
Plato's theory of forms 33
pluralism 129–30
process theology 27
Prosper of Aquitaine 7

Quest of the historical Jesus 52–54

Radford Ruether, R. 115
Rahner, K. 83–84
ransom 98–99
reason 13–17, 32, 35
Reformation 8, 144
religions 129–32
repentance 104, 145
resurrection 107, 110–12, 120, 139, 145
revelation 14, 15, 48, 61–62, 83
righteousness 106
Rocha, G. 127
Romanticism 17–18
Ross, S. 148
rule of faith 10

Sabellianism 74
sacraments 148, 155
sacrifice 99–101
salvation 20, 61, 89–112, 113, 119; universal 128–29, 131
sanctification 106
Schleiermacher, F.D.E. 19
Schweitzer, A. 114
science 17, 24, 25–26, 32, 64
Scripture 4–9, 11, 12, 71, 139
Second Vatican Council 9
sin 22, 39, 94, 96–97, 103–7
Socrates 120
Son of Man 49
Spirit 28, 29, 30, 43, 65, 77, 119–20, 140–41, 143–44; gifts of the 143–44, 153
Spirit Christology 65–66
stewardship, 31, 39
Strauss, D.F. 52
subordinationism 81
suffering 123–28

Tertullian 14, 15, 76, 104
theodicy 123
Theophilus of Antioch 14
Thomas, R.S. 116
Torrance, J.B. 37, 149–50
tradition 7–12
Trinity 70–87; economic 79–80;
    immanent 79–80
tritheism 81
Turretin, F. 16

Valentinus 33

Walker, A. 85
White, L. 30, 31
Wiesel, E. 72
Wolterstorff, N. 125
Wordsworth, W. 18, 19
worship 149–5

Zizioulas, J. 40

Made in United States
North Haven, CT
19 August 2022

22946336R00104